from the Furnace of Affliction to a Wealthy Place

"Thou hast caused men to ride over our heads; we went through fire and through water: but thou broughtest us out into a wealthy place." Psalms 66:12

Unless otherwise noted, all scripture is taken from King James Version. (KJV)

Paulette Blaylock

© 2016.
All rights reserved

API
Ajoyin Publishing, Inc.
P.O. 342
Three Rivers, MI 49093
www.ajoyin.com

No part of this book may be reproduced or transmitted in any form or by any means, electronic or mechanical—including photocopying, recording, or by any information storage and retrieval system—without permission in writing from the author, except as provided by United States of America copyright law.

Please direct your inquiries to admin@ajoyin.com

ISBN: 9781609201258

Printed in the United States of America

Contents

FOREWORD 5
INTRODUCTION 7
Chapter 1   Falling into the Trap of Fear 9
Chapter 2   The Sting of Death 15
Chapter 3   Something New and Wonderful 19
Chapter 4   The Blackest Night but Greatest Light 24
Chapter 5   Staring into the Face of Death 29
Chapter 6   I Met the Comforter 34
Chapter 7   Going Through 39
Chapter 8   Generals Chosen by God 45
Chapter 9   He Carried My Grief and Sorrow 50
Chapter 10 Don't Look Back 58
Chapter 11 When Separation Comes 63
Chapter 12 The Grave: God's System 69
Chapter 13 The Furnace of Affliction 75
Chapter 14 The Ford Jabbok 81
Chapter 15 A Wealthy Place 85
EPILOGUE 94

Foreword

After witnessing the events surrounding the funeral services of Rick and Jamie Blaylock, there are certain impressions that will forever be imprinted in my memory.

At the conclusion of the chapel service, I will never forget Paulette Blaylock coming out of the family room, approaching the casket of her beloved husband and daughter and standing to address those congregated.

As Paulette stood there, a supernatural calm fell upon the room. In my heart and spirit, I identified this as the Spirit of God among us. Appearing as an angel, Paulette flowed, as her entire being was itself filled with the Holy Spirit. The words she spoke were God's words and the message was clear.

She said we were not to weep and mourn for her husband and daughter. This was a day to rejoice, it was their graduation day! Their trials of this life were over, as they now possessed their glorified bodies and now lived in their new heavenly home.

-Ted Goode
Myers Funeral Service & Crematory
Porterville, CA

Paulette Blaylock is a person whose character has been tempered by the experience of life. Her story is one of victory and peace in the midst of incredible circumstances. I was with her when the news came that her husband and daughter had been promoted to heaven by means of a tragic auto accident. Through that sudden loss, God gave Paulette peace and a song. Only recently was she able to share with me the details of God's sustaining hand in her life.

G.A. Young wrote some words which are descriptive of Paulette's victory:

"Some thro' the waters,
Some thro' the flood,
Some thro' the fire,
Some thro' the blood,

Some thro' great sorrow,
But God gives a song;
In the night season, and all the day long."

Paulette's story deserves to be told because her ministry and message is vitally used of God to encourage others in the midst of tremendous loss. I consider it a privilege to be her friend in Christ; and commend her and her book to you.

-Joe McMahan, Pastor
Church of the Nazarene
Lindsay, CA

There are times in life when we feel that God has definitely and divinely ordered our footsteps to be in the lives of others to share in the hurts and the glories. It was a black and saddened morning when this ministry was birthed. Out of death came life. For this cause I believe that this book will be the beginning of new life for many souls.

The price of this ministry could not be measured in silver and gold, but in the love that Paulette has for God. Paulette writes as the Holy Spirit inspires.

John 12:24 says, "Verily, verily, I say unto you, except a corn of wheat fall into the ground and die, it abideth alone: but if it die, it bringeth forth much fruit."

-Pastor Dorothy Evans
Refuge Christian Center
Pasadena, CA

Introduction

My furnace of affliction began on Monday morning, November 9, 1987, at 10:00 a.m.

My husband Rick and my ten-year-old daughter Jamie, were killed instantly, in a head-on-collision with a drunken driver.

I had loved the Lord all my life, but never had I known Him like I would. He drew me so close to His heart, as He sent His Holy Spirit on that very important day.

The day of their funeral, as the Holy Spirit comforted and strengthened me, I rose to my feet, walked out in front of the casket where one-half of my family lay. There, with supernatural strength I began ministering to the people.

Remembering back to the first three of my high school years, I recall battling fear and deep depression. Those painful years taught me how to guard my mind, in the seasons to come.

Following those terrible years, came a most devastating year.

My dad fell to his death, from a tree onto a concrete patio. My brother's two children were killed in a car accident. My grandparents passed. All five deaths came within one year. So I had felt sting of death and it was an ugly, tormenting sting!

But somehow, when Rick and Jamie left us, it was different. I believe that it was because of the previous years, in training at H.S.U. (Heaven's State University) where the Holy Spirit had been my instructor. Therefore, instead of my past sufferings returning to torment me, they now begin to work for me in the hottest, most fiery furnace of my life.

I give my Precious Heavenly Father, praise daily, for the "wealthy place," that only He could have brought me to.

I pray that the contents of this book, will bring you out of your fire, and into the "wealthy place," the Lord has prepared for you.

HE'S ALL THAT I NEED
Paulette Blaylock

When my soul is crying – no light is shining,
Trouble is present everywhere that I turn,
And my heart is full of darkness and life seems so hopeless,
Here comes the Holy Spirit, bringing all that I need.

He's my strength in the weakness, light in the darkness,
I go from glory to glory; He's all that I need,
He's my stream in the desert, life's greatest shelter,
He's the rock of the ages; He's got all that I need.

He gives me heavenly power; He's got strength like a tower,
Take a drink of the Spirit, let Him cleanse from within,
He will compare to no other, let Him clothe you in His power.
Then you'll be ready for the battle, you've got all that you need.

Chapter 1

FALLING INTO A TRAP OF FEAR

"For God hath not given us the spirit of fear; but of power, and of love, and of a sound mind." **2 Tim. 1:7**

I was a freshman in high school when my older sister got married and moved out. This meant that I was next in line to claim her bedroom as my own. Finally, the privacy that I had been waiting on for years was now mine.

The first night in my new room hadn't turned out as exciting as I had planned. I turned the light off, slipped into bed and began to think over the events of my day, when suddenly my thoughts began to change. I began to entertain the thought of some dreadful disease that was going to come upon me and overtake me. I was young and innocent and did not recognize the trap that Satan had set for me. **2 Cor.2:11** states, *"Lest Satan should get an advantage of us: for we are not ignorant of his devices."* <u>I had been ignorant to Satan's devices, so he began to take advantage of me.</u>

What had started with one thought, became a **stronghold** to my mind. It took me down a very scary and lonely road for all those years. I didn't know that the Bible had given me specific instruction against this kind of fearful thinking. Later, I read a very encouraging scripture, that clearly said <u>***"Casting down IMAGINATIONS, and every high thing that exalteth itself against the knowledge of God and bringing into captivity EVERY THOUGHT TO THE OBEDIENCE OF CHRIST."***</u> (2 Cor. 10:5)

Instead of my casting the thought down, the thought began to cast me down and tear down everything that I knew about God and His goodness. **<u>God's word told me to bring that thought into captivity, but I let IT bring me into captivity.</u>**

How did I go against God's word? First, I wasn't aware of the promises that God had given to me. Secondly, I was giving attention to the wrong kind of thinking.

Paul gave us a list of things to think on: **Philippians 4:8. "*<u>Finally, brethren, whatsoever things are true, whatsoever things are honest, whatsoever things are just, whatsoever things are pure, whatsoever things are lovely, whatsoever things are of good report; if there be any virtue, (moral excellence), and if there be any praise, think on these things.</u>*"** Thinking on the opposite of these good things will rob you of your peace of mind. <u>However, it still took my young mind awhile to grasp the words, that the Holy Spirit had led me to in the scriptures.</u>

Fear began to rapidly grow in my mind. Night after night; I thought on those tormenting thoughts until they began to carry over into my day. The thought of a sickness coming upon me began to occupy most of my thinking. I became scared and depressed. I began to have frequent panic attacks and phobias that I didn't understand. Many times

during school hours, I felt as though the walls were closing in on me. My tongue felt thick in my mouth, my hands were cold and clammy, my heart began to pick up its pace, pounding so hard I thought surely someone would hear it. I felt as if I were going to fall out of my chair. I would rise to my feet very quickly in a panic, and go to my teacher and ask her to please dismiss me from class. I would then make my way to the school nurse, to get released to go home as soon as possible. This would happen to me two to three times a week.

It was such a horrible dark pit, that I found myself in, and I had no idea when, or how, I would ever get out. <u>It seemed so dark and hopeless</u>. I really thought I had no control over my mind. I didn't want anyone to know how miserable I was. I really thought I was losing my mind. However, I hid my problem very well during that time to my friends and family. I felt so humiliated and embarrassed when I went to church because I knew that I was defeated within myself.

My precious mom and dad were always there for me. They tried to talk me out of my fears and it helped only for a few moments. But they still had no idea how bad off I was.

The **<u>STRONGHOLD HAD SEEMINGLY TAKEN OVER MY MIND.</u>** <u>When I spoke with a friend, I really didn't hear a word they were saying, or when I watched TV, I didn't seem to be able to see or hear it.</u> **It was as though my mind and thoughts were paralyzed.**

My stomach began to feel the stress of my mind. My appetite left and I could hardly force anything down except maybe some fruit and a small glass of milk. I was 5'7" and weighed about 90 lbs. The nights became very long. How I dreaded to see the evening come. My only dream was that someday I might get free from this prison. I just wanted to be like my sisters. My sisters seemed so happy go lucky and did not worry about anything. I just wanted to be a normal, carefree teenager. I just wanted to laugh, just once!

The Day I Had Longed For

After those three-and-a-half years in a darkened cave, light began seeping through. **Isaiah 60:2** began to live: **"For, behold, the darkness shall cover the earth, and gross darkness the people: but the Lord shall rise upon thee, and His glory shall be seen upon thee."**

I was always very faithful to my parents, my church, and my Heavenly Father. We had youth night at the church on Wednesday evenings. However, I had no idea a new beginning was just ahead of me. I would finally walk out of this lonely, darkened cave. The minister had finished his message that night, and I can't remember one thing that he spoke about. But how I remember what the Holy Spirit did! He gave my Pastor a word of knowledge. Pastor said, "there is a young person present, who had been living in a state of fear and depression for a long time, and if that person would come forward, God would set them free." He didn't have to repeat for a second time. I immediately left my seat and walked to the front to receive what was rightfully mine. Thank God, I obeyed!

<u>God began a healing process in me that night</u>. I'll never forget the strength and joy that began to flow through me. I now realized that God knew my name and He had known what I was going through, and He was going to help me. Within 2 weeks of that night, I was totally free.

One day my pastor came to our home to visit my parents. He never really knew the depth of what had transpired that night. I briefly mentioned to him about the fear that had been upon me and the healing that had taken place. He then introduced me to a scripture **"Our soul is escaped as a bird out of the snare of the fowlers; The snare is broken and we are escaped**!" (Ps. 124:7) That was me! Praise God! The scripture the pastor read to me went off inside me like dynamite,

2 Tim. 1:7: **"***For God hath not given us a spirit of fear; but of power, and of love, and of a sound mind.***"**

The "love" didn't say much to me, the "power" didn't seem to impress me too much either, but when he read a **"sound mind"** that's when the dynamite of deliverance exploded within me!! "That's it, that's it, my mind was yelling within me. "That's what I've been looking for and it's available, to me?   In fact, it belongs to me." A sound mind! Almost too good to be true!

My life began to change. I began to laugh at things people would say. I mean, really laugh! It wasn't fake or forced. How I enjoyed laughing and really hearing, what people were saying.

I soon realized how selfish I had been. My mind was totally upon myself and the fear. When your mind is so full of one thought, you will not get interested in anyone else or anything else. The Lord revealed to me, that not only had I been selfish during those years. I had also been deceived by Satan. I had fallen into a trap that he had set for me. Now I warn you, with the same warning Peter gave us, in **1 Peter 5:8:** *"Be <u>sober</u> (self-controlled, sober-minded), be <u>vigilant</u> (watchful); because your adversary the devil, as a roaring lion, walketh about, seeking whom he may <u>devour</u> (to eat; swallow)."*

<u>You must guard your mind, for this is where the battlefield is.</u> If you allow intruding thoughts to linger in your mind, then they will set up housekeeping in your mind. It will become as their own property, and will begin to rule your flesh. You cannot give them a place. **Eph. 4:27,** *"Neither give place to the devil."* <u>If Satan can get you into depression, he will use it as a stronghold against you! He knows that you will not be able to function as the man or woman that God has called you to be.</u> If you are depressed, you will not be able to father your children as the priest of your home or mother your children in the capacity you should.

It will rob you of the joys of life. **John 10:10,** *"The thief cometh not, but for to steal, and to kill, and to destroy: I am come that they might have life, and that they might have it more abundantly."* <u>God's plan for us is that we might live in 100% VICTORY.</u>

God knows nothing about fear, because *He is love.* **1 John 4:18** – *"There is no fear in love; but <u>perfect love</u> casteth out fear: because fear hath torment. He that feareth is not made perfect in love."*   If you are fearful, ask God to shed His love abroad in your heart. He promised to do it for you **(Rom. 5:5)** *"And hope maketh not ashamed; because the love of God is shed abroad in our hearts by the Holy Ghost which is given unto us."*

Please know this one thing: <u>no experience that comes into our life is useless.</u> Make it work for you! According to **Romans 8:28,** *"And we know all things work together for good to them that love God, to them who are called according to his purpose."* It will work together for your good. I am totally convinced of those inspired words.

That lonely desert of darkness, in my mid-teen years taught me so much. <u>That experience alone, has, aided me in so many other situations.</u> It taught me to <u>GUARD my heart and mind</u> with the peace of God. **(Phil. 4:7) "And the PEACE OF GOD, which PASSES all understanding, shall KEEP YOUR HEARTS AND MINDS THROUGH CHRIST JESUS."** Someone once said, "You can't keep a bird from passing over your head, but you don't have to let it make a nest in your hair."

I've been able to minister to many who have lost control of their minds to fear, depression, and other things, because I have been there. <u>Personal testimony is one of the greatest messages of all.</u> It helps us and others to overcome the enemy. John said, in **Revelation 12:11,** *"And they overcame him by the <u>blood of the Lamb</u>, and by the <u>Word of their testimony</u>; and they loved not their lives unto the death."*

<u>Use your testimony to tear down strongholds in the lives of others</u>. Also use it, to guard yourself, against reoccurrences of similar things coming into your life. <u>You must intentionally guard your mind against Satan's devises.</u> What a boot camp of training that I had just completed! But only through Jesus!
Phil. 4:13 *I can do all things through Christ which strengthens me.*

I WANNA GO TO THAT CITY
Paulette Blaylock (1st song written, at age 13)

When I travel down the Road of Misery
When I'm troubled with fear and doubt,
I think of my home over yonder,
That my Bible tells me about,
Why worry about tomorrow,
It may not even come about,
The Savior will come for His people,
That's when we're gonna sing and shout.

I wanna go to that city, yes I wanna go over there,
He's gonna show me all around that city,
and I'm not gonna have a care,
I'm gonna sing and praise His glory,
As we walk along the streets of gold,
We'll live forever and ever and our lives shall never grow old.

Jesus has always been my everything,
He is my everything,
I feel His hand of mercy, He has set my poor heart free,
If you're not ready, all ready to go,
Just seek the Savior, He'll pardon I know,
A long time I've waited, we've all waited I know
Still He is my everything.

Chapter 2

The Sting of Death

"But I would not have you to be ignorant, brethren, concerning them which are asleep, that ye sorrow not, even as others which have no hope." (1 Thess. 4:13)

It was 1968, I was now a Senior in high school and enjoying my new freedom of mind. Another tragedy visited my family which took my mind even farther away from the fear and selfishness I had possessed.

I was in my English class when a messenger came and called me to the administration office. When I arrived, my cousin stood there with terrible news for me and my sister, Judie. He told us that our oldest brother, Larry, had just lost both of his small boys in a car accident, a head-on-collision with a school bus. He also said that Linda, our sister-in-law, was in the hospital in very critical condition. The babies were Larry and Linda's first and only children, ages four and two years of age.

The words were very great and stung too bad to describe. My brother came to know the Lord that day. His hurt and pain were beyond mention. His wife lay near death and both baby boys were gone. How our hearts broke for them!

Soon Linda began to come into consciousness. She asked for her boys and if they were okay. Larry had to tell her they were now in eternity and the funeral was past. What a horrible emptiness and agony they must have experienced at that moment.

It took many years but somehow God in all His wisdom began to heal and restore their lives. He did what no doctor or person on this earth was able to do and that was to mend their broken hearts. About a year later, they gave birth to a precious baby girl. Only our Father knew what they needed and how to restore their hope when it seemed that all hope had been taken away. Death seemed to move in on our family in that year.

My grandfather had died just before Linda's accident. Then a few months after losing Grandpa and both boys, my grandmother died. The heaviness was great in our home.

My father was a very quiet man. He kept his emotions hidden, but soon he developed bleeding ulcers and was hospitalized. The sting of death was at a high level raging inside of him. He just couldn't deal with the loss of his grandsons and both of his parents.

It seemed like after a few months we began to feel some peace in our home but then like a hurricane the wind of pain blew again. I was still in my senior year of high school and in spite of all the losses; I was excited to see my mind had remained free of fear and depression. Again, my sister and I were called to the administration office from our classes to hear the fatal news: our precious daddy, age 46, had fallen from a tree twelve feet onto a cement patio. They quickly brought us home to our mother, where they were waiting for us so we could all go to a Bakersfield hospital. Our father's condition was very critical and they were transferring him from Porterville to Bakersfield. He was in an unconscious state. The saints at home were praying and we were there pleading and begging God to spare his life.

I recall one incident in particular that gave me a great lesson that I'll never forget. I had gone to the pay telephone to call my pastor's wife at home in Porterville. I wanted to make sure they were praying and believing with us. When I returned, I told my pastor, who was at my father's bedside, that God had told me daddy would live and not die. Thank God for the man of God who spoke in boldness to a young girl, even in my hurt. He seemed to scold me! His words were very gold as he said, "No, Paulette, no, God did not tell you that. That is what you want to believe. If God spoke it to you, that's fine but if not, satan will use it to hurt you later." After twenty-four hours, daddy went on to be with the Lord.

We cried, moaned and rebelled against God's plan. I didn't care whether it was His plan or not, I felt like He had missed it on this one. How could God take him from us, leaving our mother and six children, three girls still at home? How could He take him from my brother who had just lost his two baby boys? Didn't God know we needed our dad? Didn't He care?

Our church family came in when we arrived home from Bakersfield after hearing the news of my dad's death. They began bringing food and compassion as well, into our home.

They would tell us such things as "He is better off now" and "He is in heaven and everything is wonderful for him." That didn't matter to us at that point. I remember how rude I thought the world and its system was. I thought somehow it should all stop for such a time as this but it didn't, life went right on.

The first night we went down to the funeral home I felt like my legs would collapse as I approached his casket. I'm sure I wasn't alone in that feeling. It seemed so unfair, as I looked into the face of a man who had always put his wife and family first and love us so much. It looked as if I could have said, "Daddy, get up" and he would obey. I felt a sudden urge to pray. The slumber room was full. All six kids and spouses were there so I found an empty space at the head of his casket and knelt down and began to pray.

I was all alone with the Lord, though the room was packed. I prayed a very simple little prayer. Through my tears, I simply said, 'Help us, Jesus." Suddenly the peace that passes all understanding became mind (**Phil. 4:7**). The peace of God was so real to me that I felt guilty many times for not grieving like the others. I questioned God, "Didn't I love him as much as the others did?" I knew that I love him as much but I would then remember how I asked Him to help me and how quickly the help came. The peace rode over the sting of death.

Even though we were Christians, we had missed the blessing in death. All we were able to feel was the sting. *Why? Because we had been ignorant of what God's word provided for us.* "**My people are destroyed for lack of knowledge.**" Hos. 4:6.

I saw it written by Paul, "**But I would not have you to be ignorant, brethren, concerning them which are asleep, that ye sorrow not, even as others which have no hope.**" (**I Thess. 4:13-18**) God made provision for us. He doesn't want us at death to act like the heathen who have no hope. He said, "*Sorrow not*". He wouldn't have spoken these words if He could not make it possible for us. These verses got into my heart and kept me free from the sting of death in years to come.

The hurt I was now experiencing was from watching my widowed mother suffer. My bedroom was next to hers and many nights I would hear her crying, missing her companion of twenty-six years. The sound would tear at my heart while I prayed for her peace to come, as it had to me and take away the widow's lonely cry. Thank God, He then began to restore and heal my mother's wounds and hurts over the coming years. Fourteen years later she remarried.

I'm thankful that God only lets us see moment by moment. Little did I know that a few years later I would feel both my mother's "widow's pain" and my brother's pain that comes from the loss of a child, all at the same time.

Chapter 3

Something New and Wonderful

> *"Who satisfieth thy mouth with good things;*
> *so that thy youth is renewed like the eagle's."* (Ps. 103:5)

The same week as my father's funeral, a friend of mine stopped by my home and invited my sister and me to go to a football game with her. I really wasn't in the mood, but with a little coaxing from her I went along. Even with all the losses that year of family members, it felt so good to have a sound mind and enjoy life again.

We arrived at the stadium and found our place on the bleachers with all the screaming Pirate fans. I suddenly noticed an attractive, tall and well-built young man standing at the rail. He had stopped to watch an exciting play. About the same time that I noticed him, my friend Dianne yelled at him to join us. I discovered he was the sailor I had been writing to while he served in Vietnam on a naval ship. His mother, one of the most precious Christian women in our church, had asked me if I would write to her son. Two other mothers had requested the same and I had written to their sons also but for some reason I had only continued to correspond with Rick.

I had never seen him in person before this night; he was home on weekend leave. He didn't bother to look me up when he came home because his mother had chosen me for him and furthermore, I hadn't cared that he didn't look me up for the same reason. That night after the game, Dianne and my sister, Judie, had told Rick that they had no room for me in the car and could he drive me home. "Of course," he answered politely, and we drove off in his '63 Chevy.

He was such a gentleman and such fun. He asked me if I would like to shoot rabbits with him the next day and I thought that was a great idea. I had never gone rabbit hunting on a first date. He picked me up about noon the next day with another couple and what a great day we had! Meeting this man was the greatest thing that had ever happened to me. He taught me how to enjoy life. He was not living for the Lord when I met him. He had been raised in church all of his life, by Godly parents, but later began to stray far away from what he had been taught.

The third Sunday he went to church with me, I had promised the Lord the night before that if Rick didn't give his heart to Him this Sunday I would give him up and not date him anymore. I had only known him for three weeks and he treated me with such respect and kindness but I knew I couldn't continue seeing him if he didn't come to know Jesus. That Sunday morning the invitation was given and he rose to his feet and walked to the front to change his life forever. That Sunday evening the Lord filled him with His Spirit.

After church he caught the Greyhound bus back to San Diego to report back for duty a changed Navy man. The following Saturday my new sailor came home again, ready to learn more about his new life. To all the single people who are reading right now, let me say to you, you do not have to compromise with the opposite sex to gain their love. Most of the time what you compromise to get, you will wind up losing, because it was upon false pretenses that you tried to gain your desire. If you love the Lord, then seek Him first and all these things shall be added unto you. **(Matt. 6:33)**.

Rick was five years older than me and the thing that really drew me to him was his maturity and the integrity of his character. However, I had not been "around' as he had and I was very naïve. I certainly didn't know what love was but he was very much in love with me and I knew it. I admired him so much but I just didn't love him the way he loved me. Rick was so patient with me and my immaturity. He said he would wait for me to love him. He waited four years on me and we had great times together. I knew I wanted to spend the rest of my life with him but I needed to love him first.

After four years, one afternoon we had a quarrel and he left me and didn't come back for eight or nine months. He even dated other girls at my suggestion and a bad one, I might add. But when I saw him with someone else, my heart began to change. I realized maybe I had loved him all along without even knowing it.

My sister had just come from Texas and had called Rick over to our home to see her. I was out that evening and when I came in and saw him seated there on the sofa, it was as though I had never seen him before. He was a brand new man; I saw him through the eyes of love. I walked him out to his car and told him I loved him and I think he went into shock.

Three weeks later at Christmas, we were engaged. One year later we married on December 1, 1973 – the most wonderful year of my life. Three years later, we had our first daughter.

Falling In Love with My Children

None of my friends bothered to tell me how you fall in love with your children but when Jamie came, she brought us into a deeper, richer life. She was God-sent and so precious to us. Two years later we had our second daughter, Sara, and the joy was repeated for the second time. I recall worrying, just a little, about having enough love for Rick, Jamie and now Sara. I thought perhaps either the new baby would be cut short on love or I would neglect some love to Rick and Jamie but to my surprise, God had loaded me with more than enough love for all of them. What a great life we had together. We were so proud of our two little gifts from God, how He had blessed us!

He blessed us again when He gave Rick a job on a cattle ranch in the hills of Porterville. It was one of the most beautiful places in the world to live and we were paid to live there. We enjoyed being able to share our home and all that we had with our families, friends, and church family. We had two private ponds stocked with fish, two rowboats, cattle, horses and acreage for hunting that so many enjoyed. In the fall, we had hay rides and wiener roasts. The men from the church came up on Saturdays to go hunting and fishing.

After two years at the ranch, with Rick raising beef cattle, the owner of the ranch and his wife were killed in their private plane while flying over Mexico. They had hit a mountain while in a cloud covering. The owner's son then leased the ranch to us without a penny in our pockets. While we were on our way to Los Angeles to their funeral, we were listening to a preacher on the radio whom God used, very directly, to give us the following message:

"For promotion cometh neither from the east, nor from the west, nor from the south. But God is the judge: he putteth down one, and setteth up another." **Ps. 75:6,7**

We knew God was ordering our steps. He was setting us up. We both began to praise the Lord. God began to prosper us from there and teach us to profit. **Isaiah 48:17** "*Thus saith the Lord, thy Redeemer the Holy One of Israel; I am the Lord thy God which teacheth to profit* **which leadeth thee by the way that thou shouldest go.**"

Rick began to lease more land and cattle. **Proverbs 10:22** "*The blessing of the Lord, it maketh rich, and He addeth no sorrow with it.*"

We had a new two-story office (or guest house) that we called our "Upper Room." We had prayer meetings up there and how we enjoyed that place of getaway. Our visitors and guests enjoyed it as well. One morning I was in the Upper Room praying. The Holy Spirit spoke to my heart to savor every moment because I would not always have that opportunity. I didn't think too much about this comment; I just continued to obey. Another time, on a winter night, Rick had a warm, comfortable fire glowing from the red brick fireplace. He was sitting in his oversized chair near the fireplace reading, Jamie and Sara were lying on the floor playing a game, and I was sitting on the sofa studying. Again, the Spirit of the Lord spoke to me, "Notice how sweet this is and savor it. You are all here, safe, together so save these precious moments." Again I soaked up the moment. Praise God, they didn't pass me by.

Now we had been married fourteen years. Rick was forty; I was thirty-five; Jamie was ten; and Sara was seven. After fourteen years of marriage, we had our ups and downs just like any couple but we came through victorious over every battle. We never lost our love for each other and with the years our love and respect increased for each other and our girls.

I'm so thankful we cannot see into future. If I had known what kind of storm lay just ahead for my family, I would have dug a hole and said, "Somebody cover me up." I would not have wanted to live.

Cast Thy Burdens
Elayne Hawkins

To the one who has no hope
There's a song I must sing
And to the one whose heart is broken
There's a message I must bring
And to the one who feels like living
is just too much to bear
I know someone who'll help you
For He's always been right there.

He's saying cast thy burdens upon me
And I will sustain thee,
For there's nothing that my blood
can't wash away
And I know sometimes it seems
There's no one there to love you
He's saying, cast all your burdens upon me.

Chapter 4

The Blackest Night but the Greatest Light

*"He shall not be afraid of evil tidings:
his heart is fixed, trusting in the Lord."* (Ps. 112:7)

What a great weekend of ministry and fellowship we had in Ventura the weekend of November 7th and 8th, 1987. Rick, myself, my sister Elayne, and her husband, Doyle, were singing and ministering on weekends together at this time. However, I did not realize this was to be my last weekend with my husband and both our girls.

What wonderful memories I have of that time together! We left our motel late that Saturday night and walked across the freeway to the beach. We watched the girls play on the sand and the beach playground equipment. The wind was crisp that night and there was freshness in the air. Holding hands, we walked back to our room; it was now time to rest up for the following Sunday morning meeting.

That morning the Lord gave me a very special message on the family of God; something I really hadn't given much thought to but by the following day I saw the message in action. We drove in late that Sunday night around 1:30 a.m. We had permission from the school to bring the girls in late on the Monday mornings due to travel and ministry. I had no idea how that Monday would unfold for me and my family.

Sara, my youngest, awoke early with an asthma attack. I tried to call my boss to tell her I wouldn't be able to work at the Bible store that day because I needed to keep Sara home. However, I was unable to reach her by phone. I went into the bedroom to ask Rick if he would be able to stay around the ranch and keep Sara. His response was that he was sorry but he had much to do that day. I then decided to take her to work with me and he would take Jamie to school.

I went into Jamie's room to wake her up. Every morning she would crawl off the top bunk and get onto my back and ride into the front room where I would lay her on the sofa.

At this point, the story in the Bible about the men Jesus told to get into the boat seems to relate to my family on this Monday morning of November 9th, 1987.

In Mark's gospel, the sixth chapter. Jesus constrained his disciples to get into the ship and go to the other side. The wind was contrary to them. It says He saw them toiling and rowing. He walked out to them on the water and the wind ceased and the disciples were amazed.

Jesus constrained them to get into the boat. The word "constrained" here means "forced". He forced them into the boat knowing there was a storm ahead but He showed Himself strong to them. That morning it was as if my family had a very important appointment to keep; as if we were constrained to get going. We were off and running.

The Winds of Change Brew

The night before, on our way home, our car had acted up. Rick advised me that I would be driving the small ranch truck to work so he could keep my car for repairs. He said the truck was low on gas, so he and Jamie would follow me into town and take care of his errands before he dropped Jamie off at school. After fourteen years of marriage, he was still very thoughtful of me. He sent Jamie inside to tell me it would be just a few minutes before he would have his truck cleaned inside and ready to go.

It was almost 10:00 a.m. and we were all ready to go. He, Jamie, Sara, and I walked out together to say our good-byes. Jamie kissed me good-bye twice that morning and I had thought how special that was of her. We parted ways, Sara and I in one car and Rick and Jamie in another. They were just ahead of Sara and me when Rick pulled into the barnyard, probably to pick up something that needed to go in to the town with him. As we passed them by we would say "good-bye" for the last time.

Sara and I arrived at the Bible store ready to start work. I had stopped by the doughnut shop to pick up breakfast that morning. As we walked through the back door, I could see my brother, Larry, standing there. His face was pale and I recognized that look. I had seen it before. He was bearing bad news and I knew it was fatal.

"Paulette, Rick and Jamie have just been in a very serious accident," he said. Then he repeated himself, "It's very serious."

I had just left them thirty minutes ago; how could this be! I couldn't seem to grasp the depth of the words he spoke.

Joe McMahan, a Nazarene pastor, was in the Bible book store shopping and had been talking with my brother before I arrived. Compassionately, he stayed with us and followed us to the hospital.

While Sara and I were riding to the hospital in Larry's car, I experienced the peace of God for the second time in my life in such a powerful way. The peace that I felt when I knelt at my father's casket was the same peace I was experiencing at that moment except it was multiplied. All of a sudden the word of God came alive in me. It was pulsating with life. The words that David had written in the 23rd Psalm was breathing: "*He maketh me to lie down in green pastures: he leadeth me beside still waters…Yea, though I walk through the valley of the shadow of death, I will fear no evil: for thou art with me.*" (Ps. 23:2, 4)

Somehow I knew I was in the shadow of death now. Did you know that before there can be a shadow cast, there must be light? And Jesus was providing more light for me than I ever knew existed. I praise God for the fact that while I was walking through the valley, He instantly caused us to lie down and rest in our minds and He was leading me beside still waters. I was very calm within. There is much power and peace in the stillness of the Lord. Wherever there is a storm in the Bible, Jesus was always causing it to be *Still*.

My brother, while driving, tried to prepare my heart by telling me over and over, it was very serious. All I could feel inside me was, "Shhhhh." I had memorized a scripture as a teenager and I realized it had also come to life that day for the first time:

"He shall not be afraid of evil tidings:
His heart is fixed, trusting in the Lord." (Ps. 112:7).

Arriving at the Emergency Room

When we arrived at the hospital, there was the message I had preached the day before in action. The family of God and my natural family were there waiting on me. How precious they were. You know I could never recall asking God to come to my rescue. He was just there. He was continuously there and I knew it. How he was keeping my heart and mind! **(Phil. 4:9)**. The very darkest hour of my life, yet I had never experienced more light. I had never felt this kind of peace. I kept saying, "I never knew God was this good."

I had never known my heavenly Father in this capacity. He was so real and so very close to me. He loved my little family so much and He was so compassionate to Sara and me. He made me aware of what had taken place this morning was very special. It was His perfect plan.

I don't remember speaking too much to anyone in the waiting room, even though there were many people there. God and I were having a very intimate time together. My niece had taken Sara out for ice cream while we waited for the ambulance to bring my husband and baby to me. We waited three hours but they never came.

Heavenly Places
Southern Gospel Song
(Author Unknow)

I've drank from a poor man's cup
And I've walked where a rich man does
But these things are earthly deeds
I've been on a mountain top
And to the valley low
But when my soul needs healing
I know just where to go.

It's in those heavenly places that I long to dwell
It's in those heavenly places I delight myself in Him
I go from strength unto strength
He supplieth my every need
It's in those heavenly places
That He restoreth me.

Moses called it Holy ground
John saw it coming down
And David found it a hiding place
So one again, today I'll go and partake
Of what awaits for me
Within that heavenly place.

Chapter 5

Staring Into the Face of Death

> *"Unless thy law had been my delights,*
> *I should then have perished in mine affliction."* (Ps. 119:92)

The nurse came out to the waiting room and called my name. I rushed to follow her into the private little room with my brother and my pastor who had just arrived. The words that the nurse spoke to me were words I already knew in my spirit. She said that both Rick and Jamie had died instantly in a head-on collision with a drunken driver.

The message was massive. It was overwhelming. My brother, my pastor and I held each other as we wept together. My first thoughts were, "I'll never see Jamie become a teenager; I won't see her children; and Rick and I won't get to carry out our plans." Our dreams had all just crashed and we wouldn't grow old together. Our family had been split in half. Life was so strange at this moment. Everything seemed so final. Our loves and our lives together were complete. It was finished.

The love and mercy of God began to flow from the Throne Room down to the Emergency Room and into my heart and mind. Only God, with His supernatural strength, could bring such peace to one at such a time as this.

Sara now returned to the hospital just as I was coming from the little room and back into the waiting room. She came to me and jumped into my arms, wrapping her arms around my neck and her legs around my waist. She said, "Mom, are Dad and Jamie here yet? Are they okay, Mama?"

The only words that came to me at that moment were, "Sara, Dad and Jamie have graduated today. God let them both go to be with Him."

She said, "Both of them, Mom?"

"Both of them," I replied. My heart felt as if it were breaking into pieces as I held my crying seven-year-old, knowing that in the natural, we had a very tough and long road ahead of us.

It is amazing how quickly so many thoughts can rush through your mind in a moment of crisis. Especially when just three hours before, we were all together safe and sound. Now I had to tell the authorities what funeral home to take half of my family to.

In just a few seconds of time my mind went back over our lives together. I was recollecting when Rick was in the Navy, during our first courtship and then our wedding day, the birth of our first baby, Jamie and the joy she brought to us. I said, "Father, these moments brought me so much joy. Now I knew I must refuse to allow satan to use this to bring me misery. My memory of them will remain sweet and they will still bring me joy."

I knew that something wonderful had happened for them, even though I knew it would be the pits for us living without them. God let me know that they had kept the greatest appointment in their lifetime. "*It is appointed unto me once to die.*" (**Hebrews 9:27**)

"*To everything there is a season, and a time to every purpose under the heaven: a time to be born, and a time to die.*" (Ecc. 3:1 &2)

The words of God were still breathing and alive. I saw how precious this day was to Jesus. **Psalm 116:15** reads "*Precious in the sight of the Lord is the death of His saints.*" Those words were comforting to me.

Paul spoke in **Romans 7:23** of seeing another law warring in his members, warring against his mind. I was a witness to this scripture. My spirit was so strong and in tune with God, in tune with His word and His plan but when my natural woman showed up, I began to hurt and cry, feeling the pain and emptiness. Part of being a parent is to protect your child. I ached with the knowledge that I had not been able to shield my Jamie from being hurt. I was not there to help her or tell her good-bye. I had always been there for my husband as well, but not this most important time.

How I longed for someone who could understand both sides of me: the pain and the peace the Holy Spirit was bringing to me right in the middle of the hottest time I'd ever known. It was a great furnace of affliction.

I knew that I was now a widow and Sara was fatherless and now an only child but what do you call a parent who has last a child? It was most empty.

Because of God's faithfulness, His Holy Spirit would come very quickly to comfort me. Then my spirit would take control of my emotions and His peace would flood my soul. He was touching Sara with the same peace.

As we arrived to my sister's home, our friends, family and church family began to pour in like a multitude but again, the Lord began to minister to me one-on-one. It seemed as though there was just the two of us (Sara and I) and our heavenly Father in the whole world.

God Questions Me

Many times in our church services we sang a little chorus that said, "*This is the day that the Lord hath made. I will rejoice and be glad in it.*" **(Ps. 118:24)** It was happening, everything that I had ministered or had sung was coming so alive to me. So many times words and songs fall from our lips with no meaning at all, but suddenly everything had life.

God began to speak some very adult things to me. Light was now shining on **I Cor. 13:11** "*When I was a child, I spake as a child, I understood as a child, I thought as a child: but when I became a man, I put away childish things.*" I must now speak as a woman and think as a woman. It was time to put away childish things. It seemed to me that God was checking to see if I believed what I had been speaking.

His first question to me was, "Do you believe that this is the day that I have made?"

I very quickly responded with all my heart, "Yes, Lord, I know You made this day and I will rejoice and *be glad in it.*"

Don't think that God does not hear your husband-and-wife conversations, He does. Here's the proof:

When Rick would come home and discuss a new idea he had in his business and wanted my opinion, I would speak these words to him many times. "Honey, you are a good man and *your steps are ordered by the Lord.*" **(Ps. 37:23)**.

So the Lord heard that and wanted to know if I really believed the words I spoke to my husband time after time. That's why he asked the second very important question: "Paulette, do you believe I have ordered Rick's steps today as well?"

Again, I answered him the second time as a woman, "Yes, Lord. I believe you have ordered both his and Jamie's steps this day." Now, He must order mine and Sara's.

I felt like I had enrolled for a few more years into H.S.U. (Heaven's State University) where the tests are very tough. However, I would learn from the Greatest Professor known to heaven and earth…the Holy Spirit.

He's Coming For Me
Paulette Blaylock

I met the Comforter
In the midst of my trouble
He came my way, when I had no other
He gave me the light in my darkest night
Now I'm walking triumphant, until He comes for me.

He's coming for me, He's coming for you
The hour is approaching, what you gonna do
I'll rise up to meet Him, tell me how about you
You'd better get your house in order
He's coming for you.

He gave me the good life
With a great family
Then He came and He took back
What He wanted from me
It's part of His plan
It's easy to see
He's writing a book, while He's working on me.

Chapter 6

I Met The Comforter

"And I will pray the Father, and He shall give you another Comforter, that He may abide with you for ever." (John 14:16)

I'll never forget Sara's and my first night alone. My sister, Elayne and her husband, Doyle, had insisted we take their bedroom. They became so precious to us. They, with their two young daughters, Ashley and Courtney, became our family and companions. One day Courtney came home from school with a picture she had drawn of her family. She had included me, with all my hair and her new sister-cousin, Sara.

The first day without Rick and Jamie was the longest day in history for us. That first night alone, together, Sara and I began to discuss what had happened that morning. We cried and we laughed as we stayed very close to each other that night and the days and nights to follow.

For about one year before the accident I felt a craving in my spirit to pray. I spent many days praying and fasting. As soon as Rick would go to work and the girls were off to school, I would clean my house and off I'd go into the rolling hills and oak trees to pray. I spend hours a day alone with the Lord. It was just something I wanted to do, as well as feeling the need to do so and not really knowing why. Many times I would stack rocks to make an altar before the Lord to remind me of certain prayer I had prayed. I saw many results due to that year of prayer. I learned from that time to this that every day must have a season of prayer somewhere in it to keep a fresh supply of joy flowing within us.

I recall, about three weeks before the accident, I was praying and I began to cry out to God to please show me his Holy Spirit. Jesus said in **John 16:7, "Nevertheless I tell you the truth;** *It is expedient for you that I go away: for it I go not away, the Comforter will not come unto you; but if I depart, I will send him unto you."*

As I was praying, "Father, I was filled with the Spirit when I was about eighteen years of age. After that fear and depression left me. However, I don't think I know this Holy Spirit or Comforter the way You want me to know Him."

How I wanted to be personally acquainted with the Holy Spirit Jesus had promised to give me! This prayer was prayed about three weeks before the accident. The first night that Sara and I lay in our bed, I met the Comforter in a very special way.

When Jesus addressed the Holy Spirit as the Comforter, He spoke of Him in the fullness of His name and character. He stayed with me all night long and comforted me as well. He brought many things to my remembrance, just as Jesus said He would in **John 14:26**. He began to show me the strengths in my husband's character. He began to reveal to me the completeness of Jamie's days and how she had finished the work she was sent to do. He ministered to me concerning life and death, heaven and hell, God and satan. How real was God's entire plan for me!

The work of the Holy Spirit is to reveal Jesus to us. **John 16:13** reads, "*…When He, the Spirit of Truth, is come, He will guide you into all truth: for He shall not speak of Himself; but whatsoever He shall hear, that shall He speak: and He will show you things to come*." Verse 14 says, "*He shall glorify me* (Jesus)." God sent the Holy Spirit to us so that we would not be ignorant concerning the things of this life. The Holy Spirit was letting me in on the eternal plan that was unfolding in my family's life. He said Rick and Jamie had fought a good fight, finished their course and had kept the faith (**2 Tim. 4:7**), so Sara and I must do the same.

It is too often that the children of God come face to face with a difficult situation or tragedy and behave as those who have no hope. What good is our salvation to us if there is not a difference between us and the unbelievers? Salvation must make a difference in your response to a bad situation.

Read **Isaiah 43:2** (**Living Bible**) "*When you go through deep waters and great trouble, I will be with you. When you go through rivers of difficulty, you will not drown! When you walk through the fire (furnace of affliction) of oppression, you will not be burned up the flames will not consume you. For I am the Lord your God, your Savior, the Holy One of Israel.*" When God said this, He was not teasing us with words. Remember, He spoke the universe into existence by just speaking His words day after day for six days.

If you will let these words of God come alive in your spirit, they will drive the darkness right out of your life. I'm a witness to this fact. I can tell you it's true because it happened to me when I was staring right into the face of death and from the natural side it looked like all hope was taken away. My husband, my foundation, had been pulled out from under me and it looked as if I was headed for a fall but because of His word, He increased my hope. Through Jesus, I was able to respond to the spirit during the hardest time of my life instead of reacting in the flesh. Reacting in the flesh will kill you!

I Saw a Lamb

Two years before this, I had a dream. I saw a little lamb that had been stripped of its wool. The lambs inward parts were exposed. I could see it was covered with blood; however, the blood wasn't dripping. It was on the Lamb's body. Then, I could see its muscles. Every muscle was intact. That was the entirety of the dream.

The next day I mentioned it to my husband and his friend. I had no interpretation of the dream but I felt that it was significant. Our friend said possibly it was a warning not to bring a reproach upon the Lord or His church; or be watchful, that maybe someone else was going to bring a reproach upon Him and He wanted me to pray concerning that. A few months after my dream, two of our top Christian leaders fell. I thought maybe that's what the dream was referring to and that I was to pray, but I really couldn't understand why God would concern me with that.

Finally, two years later, the Holy Spirit interpreted the dream for me. It was a short time after the accident and I was sitting in my sister's back room crying and my heart was aching. Suddenly, my spirit perked up. It resembled a dog sitting up and putting his ears straight up to hear! My spirit-ear was opened to the voice of the Holy Spirit and my heart stood at attention to hear His message.

He said, "The lamb you saw a few years ago was you. You have been totally stripped. Rick, your protector, is gone but I will be your ultimate protection. As you saw the lamb's blood, so people are looking at you. They can see the hurt but they don't see you dripping in it. Because of My blood, they will see My strength made perfect in your weakness. As you saw the lamb's muscles intact, so will they see My muscles (strength) in you."

Hallelujah! Oh, the love of our Father to us! He knew years ago what I would be facing and He put me in training years before. The book camp of fear and depression and almost losing my mind was a very hard obstacle course but it taught me how to keep my mind when harder times came. The sting of death five times in one year taught me to look only to Jesus, not at the hopeless situation. My entire family experienced all these deaths as well but He taught me through it because He knew there was more to come for me.

We never go through the University of learning that we don't come out a winner as we will apply the teaching. If you go into your training or enter your school whining all the way, then when your next test comes, you'll be overcome by it and you will lose and not win, because of your murmuring and unbelief. That is an absolute proven fact. Like the children on Israel they were broken off **(Rom. 11:20)**. Murmuring is a very deadly weapon against your victory, according to

I Cor. 10:10 *"Neither murmur (to complain) ye, as some of them also murmured and were destroyed of the destroyer (satan)."*

Take an example from our teacher, Jesus. **Luke 4:1** *" And Jesus being full of the Holy Ghost returned from Jordan, and was led by the Spirit into the wilderness."* (His school of learning H.S.U.) Notice: He went into the wilderness full of the Spirit and He came out in **Luke 4:14** full of power. If you will stay prayed up and full of the Spirit, it makes it much easier in your wilderness. You won't behave as others who have no hope and you will come out of your wilderness full of power, just like Jesus did.

Jesus did it so we could do it. He made it possible for us to walk in 100% victory just as He did. Proof: **I Cor. 10:13** *"There hath no temptation taken you but such as is common to man: but God is faithful, who will not suffer (permit) you to be tempted above that ye are able; but will with the temptation also make a way to escape, that ye may be able to bear it."*

Remember this: However you go into your wilderness, that's the way you're going to come out. If you go in "full", you'll come out "full". If you go in "empty", you'll come out "empty". It's up to you. You can choose!

I was right in the middle of a wilderness. People were asking me, what are you going to do? I just kept doing the only thing I knew!

I'm Going Through
Paulette Blaylock

In the hour of my greatest loss
When I carried my heaviest cross
When I walked through the valley of death
He restored my soul, as I took my test
As I walked down the uncharted path
How I was shaken and under attack
But my warrior came bursting through
He let me know that I would get through.

Now I'm goin' through
Yes, I'm goin' through
Through the field of losses and crosses
I'm goin' through.
Tho' the weapons were formed all around me
They could not prosper, I could not be moved
Then I heard the great commission,
Rise up, yes you're going through.

Satan comes to buffet the way
To make you weary and cause you to stray
Don't be passive, but declare the attack
Just go to war, don't ever look back
The anointing will break every snare
In this warfare, there's no reason for fear
Keep your eyes, keep your eyes stayed on Jesus
And keep lookin' up and you'll make it through.

Chapter 7

Going Through

> "When thou passest through the waters, I will be with thee;
> and through the rivers, they shall not overflow thee:
> when thou walkest through the fire, thou shalt not be burned;
> neither shall the flame kindle upon thee." (Isaiah 43:2)

My seven year old, Sara, read the Psalms to me at night and the Proverbs she read to me in the morning. This mountain of loss was so huge I couldn't even focus my attention long enough to read the Word or to pray; but when my Sara read to me, it was like a healing balm. This is when I began to see how much prayer and Bible reading I had deposited into my account. It's so important to store up the Word of God and prayer for the time of famine and when the battle is too hot to see, it will carry you through. Somehow you begin to draw out of the account and what an overwhelming victory it is.

The words of Peter had a most peculiar ring to them as I recall to my memory **I Peter 4:12**: *"Beloved, think it not strange concerning the fiery trial which is to try you, as though some strange thing happened unto you."*

My husband and baby were gone, my family had split right down the middle and he says think it not strange? I mean, it was very strange. Two days ago, I had a normal home and family of four and now my life along with Sara's was turned upside down.

The Winds of Change Had Blown

As the old saying goes, I couldn't see the forest for the trees. My mind was so foggy, yet my spirit was so clear. Thank God that my spirit was in tune with God. When this is true, then you will be able to see hard times from God's view point. You may not understand it but you will be able to accept it. With my spirit in charge, I was able to trust in the Lord with all my heart and did not lean to my own understanding **(Prov. 3:5)**. I had no understanding to lean on anyway.

The night before the funeral, Sara began to miss her daddy. She cried violently for him. My heart was breaking as I held her and cried with her. I couldn't find words for the situation. What could I say? However, in just minutes, I felt the Comforter come to us and pour the sweetest peace upon both of us. We had many of those times together alone and the Holy Spirit was always on time. He is always a perfect gentleman. He always seemed to give us the time to cry because He knew we needed the release; then He would dry our tears. Oh how we needed Him and thank God He was there for us!

That night I was awake most of the night. My mind was so full. All night I was thinking of the funeral to come and how could anyone possibly speak the words that my Rick and Jamie deserved for their home going? All night I kept speaking at the funeral and telling all who were present about Rick and what an honest and wonderful man and husband he was. I was also speaking of Jamie and how loving and spiritually mature she was. The words kept rolling.

When I awoke that morning, Sara woke up before me and I could see her in the bathroom brushing her hair and singing, "Oh magnify the Lord, for He is worthy to be praised." The joy began to bubble up within me and I knew she was ready to face our day.

Our pastor came to our home early that morning. We sat and talked for a short time and I said to him, "Pastor, I'm not sure, but I may have something to say at the funeral this morning." He looked at me with a blank expression. "But don't plan on it because I'm only taking one moment at a time. I don't even know if my legs will carry me into the funeral home but should you see me coming, if you will just give me space."

He so sweetly answered, "Paulette, this day belongs to you and your family. Do as you please."

Sara had said to me earlier she didn't want to go to the funeral and I told her that was fine with me and it was also fine with Dad and Jamie. When the family car pulled up in front of the house to pick us up, Sara pulled me back into the bedroom and said, "No, Mama, please don't leave me. What if you get killed, who will keep me?"

I told her that I must go for Daddy and Jamie's sake. I promised her that if she wouldn't worry about me, I would not worry about her. With that, she let me go.

The Funeral

Even though Rick and I both had large families, it seemed as if I was in a world all alone that day at the funeral. A short time after we were seated in the family room, they began to play my husband's favorite song, "The Master of the Wind," which was on our new tape. An awesome peace hovered over us. People were out on the grass and sidewalk because there was no room inside. The pastor read the obituary, then they played another song off the tape, a song I had written when I was thirteen years old called, "I Wanna go to that City".

The pastor then preached the sermon. He compared Rick and Jamie to the story of Saul and Jonathan in **2 Sam. 1:23**. "***Saul and Jonathan were lovely and pleasant in their lives, and in their death they were not divided: they were swifter than eagles, they were stronger than lions***." His sermon was beautiful, very fitting and described my precious Rick and Jamie perfectly.

They played one more song with Elayne and Doyle and myself (The Sevilles) singing an old congregational song, "I'll Have a New Life". As the song began to play, (as John said in the book of Revelation) I was in the Spirit on the Lord's Day; I knew exactly what he meant. This was the Lord's Day for me. I rose up in my spirit, then rose up to my feet and walked out in front of my family's casket and began to speak. I can almost repeat what I said word for word.

I walked out while the song was still playing and began to sing with it. The people began to stand, sing and clap their hands with me. When the song was over, I told them of the song I had heard Sara singing earlier and would they sing the chorus with me. We sang, "Oh, Magnify the Lord, for He is Worthy to be Praised". The worship was beautiful and the atmosphere was thick.

Rick and Jamie were buried together in the same casket, which was closed (I wanted Jamie with her dad). Sara and I never saw them again after we said our good-byes three days earlier. On top of the casket I had among the flowers Rick's rope, hat and my favorite picture of him. Next to his things I had Jamie's Cabbage Patch doll named Freddie and her new school picture, which I had just received the day before.

I told the people that morning how Rick would tell us in his quiet manner not to make a big deal but Jamie would tell us, "Go ahead, make a big deal over us." I told them that Rick was a man's man, he was God's man and he was my man. As for Rick and his house, the Blaylock home, we chose to serve the Lord.

I remember ministering something about never being ready to give a loved one up whether they are 85 years of age or 10 years old like Jamie. I ministered to them about the completeness of their lives.

We then lifted up our voices together and said, "I love you," to both my precious husband and baby. Oh how I felt their love surge through me that day. They were and are "The Wind Beneath My Wings", as the song writer had said.

We drove on to the cemetery. When we arrived and got out of the family car, I joined hands with Rick's nephew who was a pallbearer and walked with them as they put my family upon the grave site. We were then seated nearby.

As the preacher brought the committal sermon, I looked above his head into the sky to see the glory of Jesus , which shone so bright it was almost blinding. I kept my eyes focused on Him. I could only see the glory of His face and His hair, which seemed to flow down the sides of His shoulders.

I believe something very special happened that day. I felt like I had died to myself. Everything within me changed that day. The things that used to be important seemed to be nothing now. I had buried self and many things that day.

The ceremony was over and the family and friends came up to pay their respects to me. They were so giving and precious to me. Each one loved us in their own special way. Each person brought their own strength to me. As they came and went, I began to take advantage of the situation. If I knew they needed God and His love, I led them to the Lord. That day I led thirteen people to Jesus and many others changed their lives.

Praise God, His strength was made perfect in my weakness **(2 Cor. 12:9)**. What was going on within me was beyond me! Here's a woman who could not even spend the night alone when her husband was out of town and now here I was walking in power, knowing he and my daughter were never coming back to me. This was possible because the Lord had prepared the path before me.

Master of the Wind
Joel Hemphill

My boat of life sails on a troubled sea
Ever there's a wind in my sail
But I have a friend who watches over me
when the breeze turns into the gale.

I know the Master of the wind
I know the Maker of the rain
He can calm the storm and make the sun shine again
I know the Master of the wind.

Sometimes I soar like an eagle to the sky
Among the peaks, my soul can be found
An unexpected storm may drive me from the heights
Brings me low but never brings me down.

Training for Reigning
Elayne Hawkins

The Commander is saying, "I need a few good men"
Mighty men of valor, equipped with all your weapons
But we need a time of preparation
If we plan to fight
Cause victory follows warfare
And we've got to do it right.

Now here we are, He's teaching us tactics of survival
So when the enemy attacks, we'll be ready for the battle
We're standing at attention
In the armor of the light
And waiting for our orders
So be prepared to fight.

We're training for reigning
The Lord's given us His power
And like a mighty army
We're possessing what is ours
And if you're faced with conflict
Through all the scars and pain
You'll come through a victor
If you're training for reigning.

Now God is drafting soldiers, soldiers of the cross
Who's willing, armed and ready, to fight at any cost
For only those who have endured
All the time of training
Can stand one day, in strength and say,
"I'm a soldier in reigning."

Chapter 8

Generals Chosen by God

> *"To open their eyes, and to turn them from darkness to light,
> and from the power of Satan unto God,
> that they may receive forgiveness of sins,
> and inheritance among them which are sanctified by faith
> that is in me."* (Acts 26:18)

I would like to refer to God's people as an army. He has many people in His army who will fight similar battles and go through almost the same battlefields and war zones in this life. He has a specific General for each group that can lead each individual in the group through their calamities to safety and victory.

God explains how He has chosen to set this system up.
2 Chronicles. 16:9, *"For the eyes of the Lord run to and fro throughout the whole earth, to shew Himself strong in the behalf of them whose heart is perfect toward Him..."* So He searches the earth to find the people that He can use to pioneer the way for others. A pioneer is one who charts a course or prepares the way for others to follow.

I mentioned earlier how God (before the accident) had placed the most urgent desire in my heart to pray. I actually craved time to get alone with God. I would cry out to God as loudly as I wanted to and was not disturbed by anyone or anything. I would return home refreshed hours later. It was as though I had stood beside the ocean and felt its mist blowing upon my face. In all this, He was preparing the way that lay just ahead.

A few months later, I went to work at the Bible store. As my boss hired me she strongly suggested that I read much. She said to read books on grief and sorrow, single parenting, divorce, financial distress and testimonies. So, I was faithful and obedient to her as commanded of the Lord according to **I Cor. 4:2**, *"It is required in stewards that a man be found faithful."* Even if I hadn't been commanded to be faithful, I believe I would have obeyed her anyway; it's a part of my character. I have a great respect for people who have rule over me.

After looking back, I'd say that every book I pulled off the shelf in that year was ordained of God for me. The author of each book seemed to be a special General that God had set in place in order to pioneer the way for me and help me get through this journey which would be an uncharted course for me. One of the testimonies I read six months before Rick and Jamie left us was so hurtful to my spirit but helped me the most.

A pastor's wife wrote her story about the change that came to her home. Her family of five, were going to attend a church convention out of state. They usually flew in their private aircraft to the conventions but the pastor's wife and daughter chose to drive home while her husband their two young teenage boys flew. The lady and her daughter arrived home but her men weren't home as yet. In the late hours of the night, the news came that their plane had gone down in a storm and all three had been killed instantly.

God reached out to her immediately and showed Himself strong to her. She continued to live in perfect peace. The furnace was hot but she had peace.

As I read her words, I ached for her. I thought to myself, "God, I would rather die myself than go through that." Never! I could never make it and wouldn't even want to try to make it. I would read a few pages, then put it down. I didn't even want to think about someone going through such a fiery trial.

After I finished reading the book, I lost it for months. I found it a few days after the accident under the cushion of my living room sofa. I picked the book up and, oh, how I embraced it to my chest! The story, the family, the whole thing, it was mine! What a kinship I felt with this precious General who had gone before me to prepare my way. Somehow, I knew God was helping me and causing me to rise above the raging storm below, as He had this woman of God.

I had also read a personal testimony by Rebecca Springer, called *Within Heaven's Gates*, which prepared the way for me as well. She spoke of dying and being taken into heaven and coming back to earth. She shared what she had experienced and her revelation of heaven as a real country. Again, I got the message way down into my spirit. The Lord had placed another General to lead the way for me.

Prayer: "Father, use me as a General as well, to prepare the way for someone who is hurting. I pray that You will brand the words contained in this book into many hearts and minds now and help someone hear the entirety of this message.

"Cause someone right now, Father, to rise above the storm that is raging in their life at this self-same hour. I thank you Father that You have heard me.

"Love this dear person as a father or mother, a husband or wife or child. God, whatever the love is that they lack I ask in Jesus' name that You will be that and much more to them now. Thank You Jesus." Amen.

Just receive this into your spirit and rest now. He has a rest reserved for you that you may partake of at any moment. **Hebrews 4:9**. "*There remaineth therefore a rest to the people of God*."

Please let me encourage you to share your testimony with others. Someone will stay in bondage if you don't use your past experience to bring them light. Maybe you've already gone through the situation that they're in right now. Become the General that God has called you to be so that their prison doors may be opened.

If you are going to be a General, you must choose to carry your cross. **Luke 9:23**, Jesus said, "*If any man will come after me, let him deny himself, and take up his cross daily, and follow me*."

Any time you are in a furnace, your cross will be heavy. Our crosses are all different. I have picked mine up every day for many years now and carried it with His help. My cross is living without my husband and daughter. Even yet, it is sometimes heavy but if I reject it and say "No, I don't want this cross," I will just make it heavier. Then you will get into the "God is Not" syndrome: <u>God is not fair, God is not caring, God is not hearing me.</u>

John 19:17, Jesus carried His cross on the way to His death. At one place, His literal cross got too heavy for His beaten body to carry and God sent Him Simon to help Him carry it **(Matt. 27:33)**. When my cross gets too heavy on some days, He always sends a Simon that will pray for me, talk to me or just love me and be with me. He knows what we need, because He's been there. **Gal. 6:2**, "*Bear Ye one another's burdens*."

We must choose to carry our cross and not a sword. When a band of men and officers from the chief priests and Pharisees came to get Jesus to crucify Him, Peter was angry **(John 18:10)** and drew his sword and cut off a man's right ear. In **Matt. 26:52**, Jesus said to Peter, "*Put your sword away; for all they that take the sword shall perish with the sword*."

Many people tried to influence me to pick up a sword against the drunk man who was in the accident. They seemed to want me to slash a sword in every direction. I knew that swinging a sword was not going to help my situation.

Put your sword down. It's not going to help you win that war on your job or any war. I promise you the Lord will help you carry the cross to victory.

He gave me the scripture in **Ps. 144:1**, "***Blessed be the Lord my strength, which teacheth my hands to war, and my fingers to fight.***" He did just what He said He would do.

When you choose to carry a sword and take care of things your own way, it makes everything much harder on you and very stressful. You will perish with your sword. If you choose to carry your cross you will still feel some pain but you will come through holding your head high and living in abundant life as a General.

Move that Mountain
Paulette Blaylock

He carried my grief and He bore my sorrow
He caused me to soar, with wings of an eagle
When I was walking, I didn't faint
And when I was hurting, He gave me grace
Then He moved the mountain
Right out of the way.

I'm gonna move that mountain right out of the way
I command it to go, in Jesus' name
It doesn't matter how big or small
It's not a challenge to God at all
When my vision is blurred and
I cannot see
I look to Jesus and not to my need
Then I speak to the mountain, to get out of the way.

When my world came crashing in
And my dreams had come to an end
His love came flooding in
And He held me, oh, so close to Him
God did just what He said He would do
He lifted me up to heights brand new
Then we went through the mountain
To a brand new day

Chapter 9

He Carried My Grief and Sorrow

"Surely He hath borne our grief's, and carried our sorrow: yet we did esteem Him stricken, smitten of God, and afflicted." (Isa. 53:4)

The Sunday following the funeral we had a church service scheduled in my home town of Porterville, California. The pastors called when they heard about the accident and said they would understand if we cancelled our meeting with them. When I got their report, I said to my sister, Elayne, "You tell them we'll be there. This is not a time for giving up but a time for going on."

So on Sunday morning The Sevilles showed up, without Rick on the drums and working the sound and without Jamie to direct our little girls when they got up to sing, but I told the church that my Rick and Jamie were into bigger and better things now. Sara and I had realized that while they were assisting the Army of God in heaven, preparing to come to get us, so would we work down here to help prepare this Army of God on earth to go to them.

We had two cocaine addicts saved and delivered that morning. As they saw me standing that morning ministering to their needs when I had just buried my husband and daughter the previous Thursday, they (along with other saints) saw someone worse off than they in the natural.

As I continued to minister after that day, God's strength began to grow in me. As His strength increased so did healing for my hurt as well as healing for Sara. Many began to call me to come and share with them what God was doing for me. They wanted to see God's strength in the most difficult situation.

I recollect saying to the Lord, "Please don't ever allow me to speak or look arrogant in telling of what you've done for me", because I knew I had no strength of my own. I was totally resting upon God and I didn't want to be guilty of taking any glory as if standing in my own strength. The strength and peace that I was feeling at the time was not anything that I could work up of my own accord.

It didn't matter to me who was around when I felt a need to break and cry for the loss of my husband or little girl, I just did it. When I was walking in strength, I walked in strength. I didn't worry about what people thought concerning me. I didn't want people to feel sorry for me; neither did I want them dictating to me that I wasn't grieving properly. It just didn't matter to me, except for what my Father was doing for Sara and me at the time. I was not worried about heroism! I just wanted to survive.

I began to question God with some things. First, I knew He was carrying me through this troublesome times so I asked, "Father, You have surely Borne my grief and carried my sorrow." I knew He had done this but I just wanted to know how He had. **Isaiah 53:4** had come alive in me and it was breathing.

If we ask our Father a question and expect an answer, do you know He will answer us? About three days later the answer began to come. One afternoon I received an out of town call from a lady who used to attend church with me. When I answered the phone she said, "Paulette, I am calling to see how you and Sara slept last night."

My response was, "We slept like babies, why?"

She said, "I don't understand. I thought surely you must have been awake all night. I was awake praying and travailing for you most of the night, my heart ached so badly for you."

As she spoke these words, the Spirit of God said, "That's how I bore your grief and carried your sorrow. I carried it through many of my children. She stayed awake for you because you needed the rest." How precious is our Lord!

The following day, as I was home schooling Sara, I took her to the library to test her. As we were leaving the library, I ran into my life-long friend, Carolyn, who is the librarian. This was the first time we had met since Rick and Jamie had left. She said to me, "Paulette, I was so angry at the two drunk men who were driving the other car. I was sick inside. I hated them, I was so angry."

The words that she spoke were very foreign coming from her lips. I had known her always to be gentle and kind but today she spoke in tones of anger. Again, my Father ministered to me the answer to my question. How had He carried my grief and sorrow? He said, "Were you ever bitter toward the drunk men who killed them? Did you carry hatred for them?" I answered , "No, Lord."

He said, "The reason is, I put that on my daughter, your friend Carolyn. I carried the bitterness and hatred through her so that you would not be troubled with it." My Father was so merciful and precious to me. He was so faithful, just like I had always heard He was. He was also very merciful and gracious to me when He called one of my minister friends in Pasadena to thwart off depression for me. Suzanne said every morning, when she pulled the covers back to get up from the bed, she would say, "Father, help Paulette to face her day today." Suzanne felt the depression and would ask Him not to let me be depressed. Thank God, He heard her and kept me from depression.

I could never praise Him enough for distributing my hurts and pain among His children. How He carried my grief and sorrow through them!

My sister, Judie, could not look at their pictures; however, I kept their pictures out all over the house. I knew that God had chosen her to carry that part of the hurt for me.

How thankful I am to my Father, my friends and family who will never know how important they were to me at this time and how they helped me carry the load.

A few weeks later, I was having breakfast at McDonalds' with Elayne when the passenger of the other car in the accident walked up and introduced himself to me. The morning of the accident, he was very drunk and so was the driver. However, the driver was killed instantly as well as Rick and Jamie. As the young man began to explain to me that he was the one who was in the accident with Rick and Jamie, strange thoughts began to race through my mind. At first, I wanted to reach out and touch him because he was the last one near them but he then began to say to me, "I'm sorry, Mrs. Blaylock. I'm so sorry."

Love that I didn't know I possessed began to flow out of me and onto the young Indian man. I ministered to him very briefly as he told me he was there to meet his attorney. It didn't bother me at all to know that he was there to perhaps get one half of the settlement, which we did get later. The insurance settlement was the minimum allowed and the young man received a third of the settlement, along with Sara and me. We had two deaths and he had a bummed up leg.

My sister Elayne, went out to her car. She didn't want to look at him, she told me later. The Lord hadn't touched her in the same manner as He had me. None of these things seemed to move me. I was again witnessing the Living Word. Paul said the same in **Acts 20:24**, "*But none of these things move me,* *neither count I my life dear unto myself, so that I might finish my course with joy, and the ministry, which I have received of the Lord Jesus, to testify the gospel of the grace of God."*

Birth to New Ministry

One morning, about one year previous to the accident, I was in my bedroom praying. I was praying for Rick and some decisions we needed to make. The Lord interrupted my praying for Rick with these words: "As I birthed forth a baby from Sara's dead womb, so will I birth forth a ministry form Rick's dead womb."

I said, "Father, I don't' understand. You know Rick's womb isn't dead. His salvation is as solid as a rock. He has a clean heart, Lord. His womb isn't dead."

I had never understood these words until about a year after the accident, when the Holy Spirit reminded me of what He had spoken to me a few years back. He said, "Did I not say I would birth froth a ministry from Rick's dead womb? Rick's fleshly womb is now dead and this ministry which you are laboring in now is from his womb." The ministry the past two years had exploded. I preached my first sermon briefly at the funeral and from then on I have preached every weekend at revivals and retreats for the past several years almost non-stop!

I knew I was called to preach from a young girl but would never admit it. There was nothing else but Jesus for me. I didn't want to a school teacher or nurse or attorney. I just remember wanting to be a faith woman but I would never say, "Preacher." Many churches didn't even promote women preachers. Besides, I didn't like the way women preachers sounded and it always looked to me as if they were the loudmouths and their husbands were sitting quietly behind them. Satan will do anything and paint any kind of picture to distract you from your calling. I said, "God, if I was a man I would preach for you."

My pastor put me into teaching a Sunday School class at age 14. I taught Sunday School for fifteen years. I've taught every age group. I was Sunday School Superintendent for a total of six years and served as youth pastor with my husband. We were full time janitors and at other times we served as Assistant Pastors. Rick served as a deacon for 15 years. We filled in for pastors when the church was without a pastor.

When our first daughter was born, we resigned our positions and went on the evangelistic field singing and teaching weekends. Notice we did every job except preach. I tried everything to satisfy that craving inside and to make it be quiet but I never did. The call to preach was forever there. Sometimes I felt as though the word of God was going to explode from my chest. Even with all the singing and preaching I'm doing now; I still can't get enough. God certainly did birth forth a ministry from my precious man of God.

I asked God one more question. "Father, please show me what you have done for me." I had been ministering now under a new anointing for a year but I didn't know if I was really telling the people I was ministering to what God had done for me. It was so wonderful, even I really couldn't understand what had transpired and I wanted to understand. I was surviving with abundant life without two of the greatest loves of my life and it was a mystery to me.

The Recovery Room

Then the Holy Spirit revealed two things to me as He began to unfold God's plan. First, He said, "If you had rejected the deaths, you would have inflicted much pain to yourself but because you accepted My plan and drew close to Me, it brought healing to you and Sara and caused Me to receive glory.

"The second thing you did was to enter into My recovery room very early. Immediately, you and your daughter began to recover. As a man after surgery goes immediately into a recovery room so that nurses can observe him very closely and minister to his physical body, you did the same. You entered into My recovery room immediately and I observed you, which was easy because you stayed so close to Me **(Hebrew 1:13-14). Ps 46:5,** "*God is in the midst of her; she shall not be moved: God shall help her, and that right early.*"

I so needed His assistance in the recovery room. One very special reason is when a husband and wife are joined together they become one flesh. I didn't realize how much we were until he was gone. If you will look into your own marriage right now, you will see that when your spouse is sick you hurt for them. When they are mad at you it hurts so bad because your one flesh is not in agreement but when you come together in love and you're getting along and love is flowing, everything is wonderful. It makes all the difference in the world.

Now, a part of my flesh, my husband, had been torn from me. It was a though I was cut wide open and was violently hemorrhaging. How I needed the recovery room to bring healing to my heart that had been ripped apart.

Hebrews 1:14, *"Are they not all ministering spirits, sent forth to minister for them who shall be heirs of salvation?"* The healing began and is continuing, as God's angel's minister to me.

Then the hurt went even deeper into my innermost being, the emptiness of being without my child. She came from my womb. I felt so empty and lost. How I needed this recovery room and its spiritual staff to take care of me and that is just what they did.

Dear Reader, if you will accept what is in your past and enter into God's spiritual recovery room, your entire life will be changed. The healing power of God will begin to heal you and you will feel better than you have felt in years.

I know some of you have some terrible memories of your past. Just because you say, "I accept my past" doesn't mean you like it. It's not saying you're glad it happened but it's saying, "God, it's too big for me. I don't understand it but it is a part of me. It is my past and as of right now, I am not going to reject it anymore. I am going to accept it. Now, Lord, please bring me into your recovery room." This is what I did. Let Him help you soon.

Caution! Caution! Caution! Caution! Warning! Danger! Danger! Danger! Do Not Enter! Red Alert!

I cannot express to you the danger and seriousness of dwelling in the past, whether it was wonderful or a pit. Do Not Look Back but keep pressing. **Phil. 3:13-14**, *"This one thing I do, forgetting those things which are behind, and reaching forth unto those things which are before, I press toward the mark for the prize of the high calling of God in Christ Jesus."*

"Father, would You cause this man or woman, boy or girl, who is reading this right now to be able to accept their past that they cannot change, in Jesus' name. Also, Lord, cause them to begin to recover now. Jesus, I know You will do it for them because You did it for me.

"I ask these things Father, in Jesus' name. Amen."

Come on in to His recovery room and let Him carry your grief and sorrow in the way that only He knows how.

It's your Road to Recovery!

Deliverance Is Mine
Elayne Hawkins

I hear a voice calling to me
In the midst of the storm
Saying, "reach out to me"
And don't be afraid of the trial
That surrounds you like a sea
Then just like Peter on that windy night
He picked me up and by His power and might
I can stand and joyfully say,
Deliverance is mine.

Deliverance is mine
Deliverance is mine
For He promised with every trial
He'd bring sunshine
Now we can't give up, we must not lose face
Keep lookin' up, cause help is on it's way,
And even in good or bad times we'll say
Deliverance is mine.

Now it's time that the people of God
Stand up for what's ours,
And sing a new song
For the body of Christ has settled for less
For way too long
So listen real close and you will hear
That same, still, small voice in your ear
Saying, "My child, no reason to fear,
For deliverance is mine".

Just remember in the good times or the bad times
Jesus is there.
In control of every situation or separation
And from the burdens you bear

So when Satan comes against your mind
He'll lose that battle every time
We're singin' a song of a different kind
Deliverance is mine

Chapter 10

Don't Look Back

"Remember Lot's wife." (**Luke 17:32**)

Many who are reading this today can say with me, "I had a beautiful past; I could spend all my days looking back." But let me share with you something the Lord brought to me concerning looking back.

Just before the time of Rick's death, he had signed a new lease on the cattle ranch and he had brought in several hundred head of pasture cattle to care for. The Lord showed me not to fret, that He would be my partner. I was able to finish the lease out and take care of the man's cattle without one loss to the herd. I worked very hard at the ranch that year. My step-dad helped me for awhile; then the Lord sent a couple to assist me. I also hired a couple of cowboys.

The manual labor was good for me. I remember the tears would flow like rivers as I worked. I saw my husband's marks all over the ranch. I worked and wept and called out to my Comforter for help.

One day we plowed up one of the fields of pasture and I got on the tractor to drive. All of a sudden I panicked. It was as though it had just dawned on me I was walking without my husband and daughter. I thought, "God, I can't make it!" Quickly the Spirit of the Lord began to minister to me that Peter panicked when he saw himself walking on the water to Jesus. It wasn't the water that frightened him but he saw the storm around him. The same was happening to me. The storm in my life was very scary if I looked at it. So, like Peter, I kept my eyes on Jesus. As quickly as the negative thought would come, the Comforter would replace it with a positive one.

My Father had done "***Exceedingly, abundantly above all that I could ask or think, according to the power that worketh in me***" (**Eph. 3:20**). Finally, the time came about nine months later for the lease to expire. At this time, many things transpired to release me from my beautiful home place filled with fond memories of raising our children and watching my cowboy companion prosper.

First, Rick's finest horse was found lying dead in the pasture one day. Next, Jamie's little dog, Sparky, that we had raised from a puppy suddenly disappeared. Then I walked out one day to call in Jamie's 4-H calf so I could take it to the sale and as I approached the lower pond which was stocked with fish, I looked and there lay all the fish upon the shoreline dead. A shocking sight it was to me!

I got into the truck and drove to the upper pond and all the fish there were dead as well. As I looked upon the pitiful sight, I stood and began to weep. I said, "Father, what is happening? Everything I have is dying."

He said, "It's time to go. I'm releasing you."

Finally, the day came when everything was out of the house and it was empty. Even before, with all the furniture inside and all of our clothes still in the closet, it was empty to Sara and me without her dad and Jamie but now it was officially emptied.

When we got into the car to drive away for the last time, Elayne was driving me down the hill when I heard the voice of the Lord whisper gently to me, "Don't look back! You'll turn into a pillar of salt."

I questioned, "Lord, what do you mean?" I knew He didn't mean a physical pillar of salt.

But the word came clearer to me, "If you continue to look back, your mind will become petrified and you won't be able to see where you are going. Keep looking ahead."

I didn't even look in the rear view mirror to get a glimpse of the white corral fences and the red barn-style house. It pays to be obedient to the voice of God.

The Broken Things

I realized that our lives together had been broken and shattered into many pieces. We can only see the puzzle of our lives in broken pieces all in a box but God sees the picture as a whole and He knows how to bring it together.

As I pondered all these things over and over in my mind, the Lord began to direct and teach me concerning these broken things. I went to the dictionary and I looked up the word "break". It means "to destroy a complete arrangement". My family had been broken in half and I wanted to know the fullness of the word "broken".

I'll never forget the first time the Spirit of the Lord began to minister to me concerning this. We were at a hotel on a weekend between church services. Sara and Elayne's girls came and asked us if they could each have a dollar bill so they could take it to the desk and "break" it so they could visit the Coke and candy machines.

Then, I began to see what the lord was revealing to me. Since all truths are parallel, here was the truth to breaking the dollar for the machine and the truth concerning my family. The dollar in its entirety was a complete arrangement but it had to be broken to bring the desired result, which was a coke and candy. He began to show me that my family was a complete arrangement but it had to be broken to bring His desired results. What desired results? I really don't know the end results but I have seen many changed lives and beautiful blessing because of this brokenness. I saw one woman set free in one of our meetings from a load of bitterness she had carried against God for nineteen years because her son was killed in a motorcycle crash. She wrote to Sara and me that she was totally free now and how wonderful it was.

The Blessing of Broken Things

Let me show you a few things in the Bible that had to be broken before the blessing could come. Mark Chap. 2 records the story of a man who was very sick and four men carried him on a bed to Jesus to be healed, but because the crowd was so great they couldn't get to Jesus. So one of the men said, "Let's "break" up the roof and let the cot down through the roof so Jesus can heal him."

See the blessing here? The roof had to be "broken" so the man could receive his blessing which was the desired result. The roof was complete arrangement but it had to be broken.

In **Mark 14**, there was a woman who had an alabaster box of ointment of spikenard, very precious (some of our things are very precious to us). She "broke" the box and poured it on Jesus' head. She had to "break" the box before she could bless Jesus the way she wanted to.

In **Acts 27:44** the ship that Paul and the sailors were on was shipwrecked and it reads: "*...they escaped to land, some on boards and some on "broken" pieces of the ship and so it came to pass that they escaped all safe to land.*" Do you see it? The ship had to be "broken" to bring about the desired result, that the men arrived safely to shore.

Mark 6:41 reads, *"And when He had taken the five loaves and the two fishes, He looked up to heaven, and blessed, and "broke" the loaves, and gave them to His disciples to set before them; and the two fishes divided He among them all."* Jesus couldn't have fed the 5,000 had He not "broken" the bread. He had to destroy the complete arrangement to get the desired result.

I hope you can see the blessing in the broken things. I'm sure there have been many broken things in your life but know that some great result will come from the brokenness. Just think, if Jesus hadn't suffered a broken heart, He wouldn't have known a thing about healing mine. I give Him all praise because He has been to every hard place we come to. He got there years before us and fought the battle for us so we could win. We can live in 100% victory because He made it possible.

Don't look back but look ahead to great results! When you are in the fire of affliction and the heat has been turned on high, please talk to the Lord and then listen to see what He will say to help bring you out. Even though I was in a great furnace, my Father showed me many things to keep my mind in peace and give understanding to the unknown.

His Love Abides
Paulette Blaylock

I sat staring through the window,
As broken as could be
My heart cried out within me
Father, tell someone my need
Then He reaches out to an earthly friend
And whispers tenderly
I have a child that's hurting
Please bring her need to me.

Then the darkness must bow to light
Weakness must bow to might
Nothing can separate me
From the love He's given to me
Satan is losing ground
By the word of God, I know he's bound
Nothing can stop me now
His love abides in me.

He reaches out to touch me
Like a mother to her baby
Like a husband to his lady
He reaches out to me
Then my heart begins to thank Him
For the greatness of His ways
And way down from within my soul
I give my Father praise.

Chapter 11

When Separation Comes

*"**Unless thy law had been my delights,
I should then have perished in mine affliction.**" (**Ps. 119:92**)*

My mind returns to one afternoon when Sara and I were alone. We were traveling up to the ranch in quietness. I began to reminisce about many times our family traveled this road and the four of us together singing or talking. The noise level would be high but now it was quiet. As time went by, the change in our lives became more and more real.

I began to talk to my Father with my heart. "Lord, weren't You a little bit hard on Sara and me, separating us so abruptly from them? Wasn't it just a little too hard on us, taking them both at once?

God so amazes me with His wisdom and answers to us. He speaks so detailed and very sweetly. He always speaks so the hearer will understand and with me, He always keeps it very simple. He always seems to answer me by two's. He took my mind back to two instances that would help me to understand my question to Him.

I recalled a time when Rick was rounding up the cattle and cowboys were present to help him work cattle that day. The men did five things to the calf at once:

1. Gave shots
2. Ear tagged
3. Branded
4. Castrated
5. Gave a pill to each one

The Spirit of the Lord had heard my conversation with my husband that day and now He was bringing the question I had asked my husband to my memory today. I said, "Honey, weren't you a little hard on those baby calves today, doing all those things to them at once?"

He replied, "No, it was best for the calf and for me. It works out better in the long run to do all of those things at once." Notice, it was the same question I was asking God concerning my family. Then the second conversation the Holy Spirit brought to mind. He's really very nosey; He's always listening, thank God!

I remembered a night Rick and I had gone to bed and our bedroom window was opened. Earlier in the day, Rick and cowboys had separated the calves from their mothers. As we lay there in bed, we listened to the babies bawling for the mothers and the mothers bawling for their babies. It was such a horrible sound. I said, "Honey, weren't you too hard on those babies today? They are not old enough for this kind of separation yet. Please move them back together tomorrow."

He answered, "I can't do that. This is best for the mother, best for the baby and best for the rancher."

Can you see how God was answering my question when I asked Him if He was too hard on my family of four with this instant separation? He assured me, as my husband had, that it was best for both the parents (Rick and me) and the children (Jamie and Sara) and for our Maker (God). It was needed and it was a perfect plan. Thank God, I was able to trust Him for all of us. When you question God, it serves to your advantage to ask Him questions that will help you.

We will be separated from people and many things during our course of life. Did you know that a Christian with a vocabulary of "why" toward God with everything that happens in their life will never be successful? I hear Christians saying, "Why hasn't God answered me?" I say, "Why don't you wait?" As long as you are asking "why", you have not released your faith into the situation.

When is God going to hear me? If you will trust Him and know that He hears you, then that knowledge alone will eliminate the when because you know He will. If you will keep faith that He is going to help you, then it won't matter when. I promise you He will be on time.

The same person that is forever asking why and when also, has the "Why-does-everything-happen-to-me" Syndrome. Look around you! It happens to all of us. It rains on the just and the unjust. **(Matt. 5:45).** God is not a respecter of persons.

The difference between the sinner and me is that I have a supernatural God to help me in my rain and wind and they don't. Some Christians behave just like a non-believer in their crisis: they don't take advantage of the help our Father offers to them. They react in the natural state of their mind which is usually fear and panic instead of responding with their spirit which will bring peace and understanding. Remember, you can't live abundantly with a heated and confused spirit.

I would like to feed these three powerful things into your spirit. Knowing these three things will pull you victoriously through any crisis. These three things go together perfectly as does the American hamburger, coke and fries.

1. You must seek the Lord in your crisis or decision making. Seeking Him must be done with the whole heart. When King Jehoshaphat had great armies coming against him and his people, the Bible says he "feared" but guess what he did?
   2 Chron. 20:3-4, "*And Jehosaphat feared, and set himself to seek the Lord. And Judah (his country) gathered themselves together, to ask help of the Lord: even out of all the cities of Judah they came to seek the Lord.*" Sometimes the places we come to in this life make us fearful. Come on people! Whether you know the Lord as Savior or not, seek Him, gather yourself and your thoughts together and say, "I've got to know Him and I am going to seek His help."

2. Know that He hears you. **I John 5:15:** "*And if we know that he hears us, whatsoever we ask, we know that we have the petitions that we desired of Him.*" What good would it do to seek Him if we can't really believe and know that He hears us? If you should ask the "average" Christian to describe God to you, you'll find their description of Him, very weak and powerless. Some say He's invisible and lives in a faraway place. "He's an old man that sits on a throne. He has a long white beard and is tired." Here's what God says about Himself in **Isaiah 40:25-26**: "*To whom then will ye liken Me, or shall I be equal saith the Holy One. Lift up your eyes on high, and behold who hath created these things, that bringeth out their host by number: He calleth them all by names by the greatness of His might (the stars and their number), for that He is strong in power; not one faileth.*"

Do you see it, reader: Our God has no problems and if you will seek Him and know that He hears you, He will help you. You must have an

image of Him in your mind, know that God has bodily parts. Know that:
  a. He has eyes, He has ears. **Ps. 34:15**: "*The eyes of the Lord are upon their righteous, and His ears are open unto their cry.*"
  b. He has a face. **Ps. 34:16**: "*The face of the Lord is against them that do evil.*" (It would do you a great favor to straighten up your act.)
  c. God has hands. **Is. 59:1**: "*Behold, the Lord's hand is not shortened, that it cannot save; neither his ear heavy, that it cannot hear.*"
  d. He has a body. **Daniel 10:6**: "*His body also was like the beryl (precious stone, sea green in color), and his face as the appearance of lightning, and his eyes as lamps of fire, and his arms and his feet like in color to polished brass, and the voice of his words like the voice of a multitude.*"

A friend said to me once, "Paulette, when I get down to pray and seek the Lord I feel very strange. Since I can't see Him, I feel as though I'm talking to the walls. This is why it is so important that you have an image of Him upon your mind as Moses did. **Hebrews 11:27,** "*By faith he forsook Egypt, not fearing the wrath of the King: for he endured, as seeing Him who is invisible.*"

Now that we have established the first two points in bringing you into victory in your crisis, the third will fall into place.

  3. After you have sought Him, after you know that He hears you, your deliverance or help will come. Watch these three powerful elements work together here:
     a. **Ps. 34:4** "*I sought the Lord, and He heard me, and delivered me from all my fears.*"
     b. **Ps. 34:6** "*This poor man cried (or sought the Lord), and the Lord heard him, and saved him out of all his troubles.*"
     c. **Ps. 34:17** "*The righteous cry (seek the Lord), and the Lord heareth, and delivered them out of all their troubles.*"

If you will take these three things deep into your spirit, they will change your life forever. I give Jesus the praise that I had knowledge of these things when He called Rick and Jamie home; how He held me up and anchored me to Him! The hurt and the pain was too great for my limited vocabulary to express to you but neither can I express to you the keeping power of the omnipotent One that I serve.

Is. 33:6, "*And wisdom and knowledge shall be the stability of thy times, and strength of salvation: the fear of the Lord is his treasure.*" And it was and still is my treasure. I sought Him and still seek Him daily and know that He hears me and He delivers me from my hurts, failures, pain, trials and fears.

When separation from people or things in your life comes, confusion and misunderstanding will take hold of you if you don't seek the Lord. Know you are not separated from His love. **Rom. 8:35**, "*Who shall separate us from the love of Christ? Shall tribulation, or distress, or persecution, or famine, or nakedness, or peril, or sword (great furnaces)? Nay, in all these things we are more than conquerors through Him that loved us. For I am persuaded, that neither death, nor life, nor angels, nor principalities, nor powers, nor things present, nor things to come, nor height, nor depth, nor any other creature, shall be able to separate us from the love of God, which is in Christ Jesus Our Lord.*"

Since <u>*absolutely*</u> nothing can separate us from His love. He is able to help us deal with separation that comes to us on this earth. When the grave separated Sara and me from our family, He shed light on the situation for me that I might see. How thankful I am for the revelations He gave to me.

Anticipating
Doyle Hawkins

The people all gathered and they were so amazed,,
As they watched our Lord ascending,,
To heaven that day,
Then the angel of the Lord said,,
Why are you standing here,
For the same way that you see Him leave,
He'll return again someday.

We're gonna be anticipating,
For that great awakening,
When the saints shall rise from the grave,
Anticipating, for we're gonna be leaving,
When the Lord shall come and take,
His children away.

Now our Lord shall return to earth someday,
And those that are waiting shall be caught up away,
Now, Satan he'll try,
He'll try to hold you down,
But when that trumpet sounds,
Your feet better leave the ground.

Chapter 12

The Grave: God's System

"The secret things belong unto the Lord our God: but those things which are revealed belong unto us and to our children forever, that we may do all the words of this law." (**Deut. 29:29**)

Rick and Jamie's promotion came in the wintery month of November. A few days later, it was raining outside. I walked to the garage where the garage door was lifted up and watched it rain.

I was standing there alone and I began to speak to my husband who loved the rain. "Baby, it's raining outside; I will try to enjoy it for you." I said as the tears came flowing down my face.

It was at this time that satan came with a thought of fear. He began to make it visual to me that my baby girl and her daddy were deep in the ground and how cold and wet it must be. See, he always distracts you from the spiritual and tries to bring you back to the natural. I had now left the spiritual things and began to look into the natural and that's where I get confused. I looked at the grave and all kinds of horrible thoughts tried to overtake my mind.

We are addressed in **2 Cor. 2:11**, "***Not to be ignorant of satan's devices, lest he should get an advantage of us.***" Whenever you become confused, know quickly that Satan is near, forming a war against you. "***For God is not the author of confusion.***" **I Cor. 14:33**.

I quickly returned to by bedroom at my sister's home and began to seek my Father's help in the hurt I felt. If I can encourage you who are hurting or confused right now, it would be this: very quickly depart from the place where your hurt or negative thoughts come and go to a place to be alone with Jesus. He will soon console you and revive you again. The understanding will come.

God's Systems

As I started to talk to Him about my thoughts of the grave, He began to minister to me in His still, small voice. I heard Him with every fiber of my being. His thoughts began to come into my mind. He shared with me that He had set up many systems that work consistently, pertaining to life and Godliness.

God in all his wisdom, set up the universe with a system that causes the entire galaxy to work like the ticking of a clock. He set all in motion with His spoken word and it's been that way ever since, without flaw.

He further said, "In the beginning, I set up the system of tithes and offerings to keep my work operating. With these I provided a living for My priests and kept My temple and sanctuary doors opened. Tithes and offerings are still in operation today. This system will flow throughout the ages of time to keep my plan in motion."

These thoughts encouraged me to receive the last words of wisdom He spoke to my heart. My Father began to relate to me that the grave was also one of His special systems. The grave has had a specific task to perform since the beginning. It keeps our bodies until He returns to join them together with our spirit.

I Thess. 4:13-14, *"But I would not have you to be ignorant, brethren, concerning them which are asleep (body sleep), that ye sorrow not, even as others which have no hope. For if we believe that Jesus died and rose again, even so them also which sleep in Jesus will God bring with Him."*

2 Cor. 5:8, *"To be absent from the body is to be present with the Lord."*

James 2:26, *"For as the body without the spirit is dead." When your spirit departs, our body dies and the grave keeps it until it is resurrected and the mortal (earthly) shall put on immortality* (heavenly) **I Cor. 15:53.**

What a system! When He explained this to me, He also gave me the understanding and I heard it with my spirit. How it calmed the storm raging inside! In a very short time after receiving this knowledge, I was able to use it to help somebody else's fear of the grave.

A minister friend of mine was visiting me from Pasadena, California. I had not shared what the Lord had given to me concerning His system until this time.

Bernadette and I were seated at my dining table as she began to share with me about the death of her brother who had passed on the year before. She said she had accepted his death but there was one thing that seemed to eat at her. She could visualize him lying on his back in the casket and being lowered in the grave. This picture would rise to the surface of her mind and display itself in motion picture form and torment her. Every time she thought of him, this is what she would see.

As she spoke those words, great anger against the wicked one began to rise up in my spirit. I had great compassion for my sister because I had battled a similar thing just before. I've never forgotten the sweetness of that moment. The presence of the Lord came by and brought to my remembrance His system of the grave. I prayed those thoughts over her. The Lord lifted the ugly pictures from her mind that day. She later told me that even when she has tried to see that picture she cannot. His plan is so perfect and, praise God, the old grave is doing its job but only for a while. It will have to turn those bodies loose when the trumpet sounds.

Death, Burial and Resurrection

I mentioned to Sara how that someday we should go to the site of the accident where her dad and sister had left us. She asked, "Why, Mom?" I answered, "I don't know, baby, I just thing we should." This was about six months after they had died. That thought then seemed to have left us and did not return for awhile. We had forgotten all about it, I thought!

Sara and I had gone to the gravesite one summer morning to take balloons and flowers. As we arrived, there was a man with a dump truck preparing to drop the truckload of dirt onto an open grave. As he saw us approaching, he stopped what he was doing and walked to the front of his truck to give us our privacy. The grave he was going to fill was just a few feet away from us.

As I knelt down to arrange the flower and balloons I had brought for Rick and Jamie, Sara ran over to look inside the open grave and yelled, "Mom, come here!" I felt fear rise up into my throat, afraid of what I might see and wondering what my seven year old had already seen. I quickly arose to my feet and went to her. At this point, the man left his truck and came toward us. As I looked down, I saw the cement vault that held the casket. Sara said, "What is it, Mom?"

I tried to explain to her the best way that I knew. I then asked the man, "Who is it?" He spoke very gently to us that she was a mother, a wife and a grandmother.

We felt such a peace come over us and I knew the Holy Spirit was about to teach me something. I felt impressed to watch the entire burial process. God will also prepare the hearts of the ones who are with you in a situation. Sara wanted to watch with me. I knew he had prepared her for this time, too.

We watched him fill the grave with dirt all the way to the top. Leveling it off with the ground, he packed the dirt in with his feet and Sara helped him. Then, he picked up a very heavy steel bar that had a flat piece of steel on the end of it and proceeded to pound the dirt into the ground He asked me if I would like to try it. Sara and I picked it up and set it down a few times helping to settle the dirt. The tool weighted twenty pounds and we could hardly lift it.

He then picked the grass up that was in three rolls and set it in place. He unrolled one roll and Sara and I each unrolled a roll and he straightened the grass over the grave.

This had been quite an experience for us but I didn't realize what we were experiencing until a little later. The same afternoon, Sara and I were driving up to the ranch when Sara reminded me of the words I had spoken to her months before about returning to the accident site. I felt the same strange sensation come upon me as I felt earlier when she wanted me to come and look into the open grave. I wasn't sure whether or not I wanted to go to the accident site today. I wasn't sure if I was prepared. So, I said to her, "Let's see how we feel when we get up there."
When we drew nearer, I knew the time was right. We drove to the top of the hill where the head-on collision had taken place and where their spirits departed. We got out and walked around, not really looking for anything. We found a couple of little pieces of our car. One was a piece of wording on the side or back of the car. Then we found something, which was most precious to me. It was an ink pen that I had dropped into Jamie's stocking our last Christmas together. On the pen it read, "Jesus is the Reason for the Season." We picked it up and held it. The end of it had been crushed but Sara said, "Mommy, it still writes." How that little phrase kept us when our first Christmas came after our family was gone!

We then walked over the top of the hill, holding the pen. I said, "Sara, Baby, let's release Dad and Jamie and thank God for giving them to us."

We did just that! As we lifted our hands to God at the top of that hill, God's presence came and met us there. What a special time it was! We then got back into Rick's four-wheel drive truck and went to the ranch to feed the animals and do our chores before we went back to Elayne's house where we stayed at night. We stayed in their home that first year and took care of the ranch during the day.

Two days had passed before the Holy Spirit let me know what had transpired that day. He said, "You witnessed the death, burial and the resurrection, all in the same day. You helped bury the dear lady at the cemetery and I allowed you to feel the power of the resurrection at the going-home spot at the top of this hill." It was a very peculiar sensation that day on top of that hill where the winds of change had blown on my family.

Each day He seemed to take us higher in Him and teach us more and more. He has brought many people across my path that had been here before me and could minister to me in a special way. He has sent me to people to go before them and show them the way through their difficult places.

Oh, how His system works! He sets it all in motion. He sends us forth to help each other.

Great change was upon us.

Lion in the Tribe of the Lord
Paulette Blaylock

I'm a lion in the tribe of the Lord
Yes, I'm a lion in the tribe of the Lord
He brought me like a king through the wilderness
Through the battlefield of fear and distress
No matter how rough the road may be
Or what the Devil tries to do to me
Through the raging war, I'm a lion of the Lord.

He didn't give me the spirit of fear
But lets me know that He's always near
He planned no defeat for me but He gave me total victory
He goes before me wherever I go
I know I'll never have to walk alone
He gave me power and authority, to be a lion of the Lord.

An over comer by the blood of the Lamb
By the power of the great I Am
Now I'm walking to a different beat
Pressing forward, never sounding retreat
He makes me stronger than my enemies
I'm taking ground as He works in me
Now He's clothed me in His majesty
Yes, I'm a lion of the Lord

Chapter 13

The Furnace of Affliction

*"Behold, I have refined thee, but not with silver;
I have chosen thee in the furnace of affliction."* (Is. 48:10)

A furnace is a place of suffering. By looking at it from the natural eye, it looks like a very hopeless place. Your attitude while in the furnace is a very important element to your deliverance. **Col. 3:2** tells us to *"Set our affection on the things above, not on things on the earth."*

I made a choice during my furnace to stay close to Jesus and keep my eyes focused on Him. The tragedy was a furnace burning seven times hotter than any other furnace I had been in. If I had chosen to look at my loss, I would have entered a pit of grief.

Caution: If you walk into grief and despair for very long, it will become a pit.

Grief is a luxury you cannot afford. The price is too great! However, at the time of separation from our loved ones a certain amount of grief is very normal and necessary. The tears must flow as the pain is felt. Please, don't panic every time the grief and tears pay you a visit. I recall many times that panic tried to drown me and still I experience tears from time to time. Allow me to share one specific instance with you.

I hadn't been grocery shopping at the place I had shopped for fifteen years, since the accident. It had been about a month since I had been there to shop. Just a short time before, the clerk would see me bring her two carts full of groceries to feed a family for two weeks and two little girls following close by. Now, they saw one cart, half-full. I used to buy three boxes of cereal – one for Rick, one for Jamie, and one for Sara. Now I only had one box. I felt the tears and pain welling up in me as I stood looking at my husband's Frosted Flakes and

Jamie's Cocoa Pebbles that would remain on the shelf that day. Nevertheless, I kept moving through the store, feeling similar feelings, conquering them one by one. I gave each memory the time it deserved but did not linger there too long because I knew the feelings could overtake me if I didn't overcome them first.

Do not give your hurting thoughts too much time. Keep them passing.

As I arrived at the register, the young lady and box boy were laughing and having fun. As I approached them, there was a hush that came over them. They looked at me with solemn faces in apology for my loss. God's anointing came upon me in great joy and peace as I stunned them with my reply. They stood in amazement as I told them how good God had been to me and how real He is. As the young man followed me to the car with all the sacks, he said to me that if something ever happened to his mother or dad he hoped he could be like me. I assured him he could if he would let the God that I serve help him. I took advantage of that moment to share the Lord's goodness with him.

As I drove away from the store, the spirit of pity paid me a visit as though a hitch-hiker had gotten into the car with me. I began to cry as I thought on the small amount of sacks in the trunk of my car compared to a few months ago. I began to see the pity in the solemn faces of the clerk and the box boy and I began to cry a river of tears. My heart was breaking in two. I couldn't see where I was driving, for the tear-filled eyes, and had to pull my car over to the side of the road. I thought this time I'm going to lost it; I couldn't gain control of it.

I sat there almost five minutes; then the word of God began to live in me again. The Holy Spirit is always so present and so aware of what's going on every minute of our lives. He saw me and was with me at the grocery store. He reminded me of the words of **Ps. 34:18**, "*I am nigh unto the one of a broken heart; and saveth such as be of a contrite spirit*." He was very close to me at this moment and I was not alone in the car. My tears dried up immediately and I started my car and went my way.

The Spirit of the Lord caused me to come up out of that pit and walk out holding my head up high. In **Is. 52:2**, we are commanded, "Shake yourself from the dust." As antagonizing thoughts come, they are like dust that's very disturbing to you. This is what I had to do in my moment of panic, shake myself out of the dust of the thought.

He said, "Arise, and sit down." Now, what could that possibly mean: arise and sit down? It means to get up and out of the place of torment; then you will enter into His rest prepared for you. **Hebrews 4:9**. *"There remaineth, therefore, a rest for the people of God."* Then what? In the same verse He then directs us to loose ourselves from the bands around our necks. One translation says, take the slave bands from off your neck.

Mr. Dake says in the Dake Bible Commentary, that "the captives or people taken as prisoners were locked in great steel bands around the neck". If you stoop too low into grief, satan will make sure it becomes a band around your neck so that you cannot function at all. God is aware of every one of satan's tactics that he uses to put a band around your neck but if you aren't aware that you have them, you cannot take them off.

I know and understand how helpless we feel at death because death has a definite sting. It looks so impossible to be restored to life without those you love and have spent years with. Jesus made real to me the words He spoke in **Matthew 19:26**, *The things that are impossible with me are possible with him*. Thank God for His words to us. He knew about the bands of heaviness that would try to wrap themselves around my neck while in the furnace of affliction. That's why He wrote to us to loosen yourself from them. We can only do that through Him, just resting in His love and care, trusting Him as a loving Father.

As you take your bands off and stand up free, resting in Jesus, you will be really loosed while in the furnace of affliction. Many ministries have begun in the furnace.

The third chapter of Daniel tells when Shadrach, Mechach and Abednego were thrown into a literal furnace because they would not bow to the king, that this was a hopeless place in the natural. But because they did not bow, they didn't burn. Hope was there! The Bible tells us that the king looked down into the fiery furnace and saw Jesus walking around in the fire with them. When the guards put the three men into the furnace it was burning seven times hotter than usual; the men were bound (or tied up) when they were thrown in but now they were walking around loose!

See, even though you get into a hard place, you don't have to stay tied up and bound in it. You can still move around and function properly. Do not let that divorce bind you up. I read that the fire had no power over their bodies. Why? Because their God was with them and they knew it. Know He is with you to deliver you.

If you won't bow to grief, you won't burn in it.
If you won't bow to memories of the past, you won't burn in them.
If you won't bow to fear, you won't burn in fear.

If you begin bowing to things that come into your life, they will overtake you. If you don't bow, you won't burn.

A very popular teaching that we've been exposed to in the past few years is that suffering doesn't come to a child of God. I'm not writing a book of controversy but I do believe the people of God do come into places of suffering. Remember, even though the three Hebrew men were in the furnace, it did not take power over them. Yes, you will suffer but No, you don't have to burn. **2 Tim. 3:12,** "*Yea, and all that will live Godly in Christ Jesus shall suffer persecution.*" **2 Tim. 2:12,** "*If we suffer, we shall also reign with Him: if we deny Him, He also will deny us.*"

Even though my furnace of losing half my family was very great and it overwhelmed me, it did not overtake me. I allowed God to work His perfect plan with the four of us.

Please look at this verse with me: **I Peter 5:10,** "*But the God of all grace, who hath called us unto His eternal glory by Christ Jesus, after that ye have suffered a while, make you perfect, establish, strengthen, settle you.*" If everything was rosy in our lives all the time, what would we know about the supernatural power of God? The furnace only burns things off of us that need to come off. He chose me in my furnace of affliction, **Is. 48:10.** He brought a ministry forth and anointed me with a fresh, new anointing. If you will hear Him, He is also calling you while in your furnace of affliction.

After we suffer awhile, the fire begins to perfect us. Yes, the fire hurts. You bet it does! But when you know that God is at work in your life, you can bear anything. Seeing all your faults, feeling your flesh fight the change, letting go of some personality traits, you begin to wonder what's going on inside. I had a few critics saying, "She's changed!" They weren't saying anything I didn't already know. I didn't pay attention to what they were saying. I had to get through the best way that I could for Sara's sake and my own.

You just can't go through the fire and not change, if you're willing to walk the walk of faith. The perfecting will go on until Jesus Christ comes.

Then, after you've suffered awhile, and the perfecting is going on, He begins to establish you. (The means used to effect the confirmation is the ministry of the word of God). You need to read that line again, you who are in a furnace. Establish also means: to fix, make fast, to set the truth that is in you.

After you are established you will then be strengthened. He will bind your body, soul and spirit together, and strengthen so there will be no danger of warping, splitting or falling apart. Please, let your Father take care of you. Don't rebel against Him in your affliction. He is the only one who can keep you together. It was only Him who was able to keep me from falling apart. He strengthened me. The suffering was very great at times.

Our first summer without Rick and Jamie, The Sevilles, went to Nashville to record our next tape. I decided that Sara and I would stay at the Opryland Hotel in Nashville while Elayne and Doyle stayed with his relatives. This hotel was one of the most beautiful and lavish hotels found anywhere. The elegant shops, waterfalls, gorgeous winding staircases, the entertainment and wonderful food made the hotel most unique. But I found myself rising early in the morning going out on the lanai with my coffee to watch the people walking down the beautiful little paths through the plants and under the waterfalls. As I watched the families enjoying their vacations with their children I would cry lonely tears until my shirt was wet. It didn't matter where I went, my memories were always present with me.

The fire is very hot in loneliness but as long as I could reach out to Jesus and He reached back to me, He always dried my tears. He was always quick to send me the help I needed. Then, after awhile, He begins to settle you. Oh, how wonderful it is after months, sometimes years, of everything in your life being upside down, that we can begin to settle down. Even though my life is not back to normal, being a single woman and mother, now I could feel Him beginning to settle me and settle my little girl.

Remember, warfare always surrounds the birth of a miracle and there is not birth without travail. But when He calls you in your furnace of affliction, you will travail and something beautiful will be birthed for you.

I've Been Through Enough
Janet Paschal

When I first began to walk with the Lord
I did not really trust Him
How He longed for me to understand I could
So through the valley, He led me, afraid as I could be
Till I felt His loving arms embracing me.

I've been through enough to know He'll be enough for me.
He's come through too many times
That puts my mind at ease for good
I'll stake my very life, he's gonna take care of me.
Yes, I've been through enough to know He'll be enough for me.

How could I ever doubt a God
Whose hands hold this universe,
How could I ever question His ability
There's no place that I can go, where He doesn't know
The things that trouble me, He's always aware of where I am an what I need.

I believe Him now after all these years,
He's been so faithful, he's proven to be true,
Never more could I ever question why
Cause I've seen Him work before and I know what God can do.

Chapter 14

The Ford Jabbok

*"And he rose up that night, and took his two wives,
and his two women servants, and his eleven sons,
and passed over the ford Jabbok.
And he took them and sent them over the brook,
and sent over that he had. And Jacob was left alone;
and there wrestled a man with him until the breaking of the day."*
(Gen. 32: 22-24)

One year after the accident, the lease was completed at the ranch. I then moved into my own home and discontinued to home school Sara, enrolling her into the public school's third grade class.

It was a tough year for both of us. She didn't want to go to school without her sister; and she complained that everyone else had their daddy and she didn't. How I ached for my baby! But God would come time after time and minister to us. Sara's teacher and the school staff were very compassionate and understanding toward us.

After she was in school, I was home alone during the week in between my church meetings and retreats. It was a very lonely time for me. I spent many quality hours, days and months alone with the Lord just He and I. I did not go to lunch with my friends or have much fellowship. I prayed, fasted, and fellowshipped with Him. How close we became! It really was very wonderful.

Many things happened that year that helped to bring me to this place. Our church had a split and friends and family went, each his own way. There were hard feelings and people weren't speaking to each other. I didn't want to leave the church because it would mean another change for Sara; I thought she needed to keep something the same in her life but finally; we left the church as well.

I was going through such a change within myself that it seemed that everything I did and said was backwards. I kept losing friends and church family. I had come to a place of aloneness but I so enjoyed my time getting to personally know Jesus!

After one year I began to look at what I had been doing now for months. I said "Lord, is all this time alone your plan for me or should I get a job and go to work?" He very quickly let me know the ministry would be my full-time job until He comes. I still spend much time alone with him.

One morning I received a call from a local Assembly of God Pastor. He said to me, "Paulette, I don't know you very well but the Lord put you upon my heart today and I feel He wants me to share these things with you." What he was about to say to me almost sounded as if he had been listening when I asked my Father the question. He said to me, "This place where you are right now is a very important place. It's been lonely but God has enjoyed your fellowship." The Pastor continued with these very important words: "Paulette, God wants you to know that masses walked through the Red Sea together and many walked through the Jordan but when Jacob came to the Ford Jabbok, his family went on across but Jacob stayed there alone all night and wrestled with the Lord." This is where God changed Jacob's name to Israel and blessed him.

The Ford Jabbok means a place of aloneness. It was literally a sixty-five mile stream, which made it possible to cross the Jordan River!

The Pastor said, "Paulette, God is changing you at the lonely place. You won't stay at the Jabbok forever but stay until He changes and blesses you."

I was so blessed by this message that was brought directly to me from the throne room in heaven. As we hung up the phone I went back to my prayer room to thank God and give Him praise for hearing me.

Then the Holy Spirit began to interpret this message a little further to my heart. First of all, He reminded me that at an early age I was such a worrier, which probably led me right into my teenage years of fear and depression but just as the children of Israel went through the Red Sea "together", so had my Dad and Mother gone through this sea of fear with me, loving, caring for and protecting me. How I drew on their strength until my deliverance came!

Then He reminded me how that our family went through the five deaths in one year "together" as His people had gone through the Jordan together. The sting of death is a deep, black Jordan.

I then saw how that Rick and I had suffered much financial difficulty when our Jamie continued to go through eye surgeries but we came through this Jordan together.

Once, when Jamie was a baby, the doctor told us she was either blind or deaf. We felt like we had come to the Red Sea but we walked through the sea together until she was made whole.

Now this crossing was totally different from our Jordan's and our Red Seas before. When Rick and Jamie went to be with Jesus, I was at the crossing alone. There were family and friends everywhere I looked but I was standing in this boat alone. Thank God for my little Sara but I had to comfort her and be strong for her. She was too young to share this responsibility with me.

I was at the Ford Jabbok, the place of aloneness but after seeing it in **Genesis 32:22**, I knew it was a wealthy place.

The Bible says that Jacob's thigh was knocked out of joint at this time of life. How I could relate to that! It felt like everything in my life was out of joint (place). Nothing was the same. The scriptures say that Jacob's wives and sons went on over the brook but Jacob was left alone. Suddenly, I could see that it seemed everyone else passed on over and went on with the normality of their lives but I was left alone. I give God praise that, as Jacob, I chose to stay there with God and not run away. Many times at the time of loss, a person's first reaction is to run.

The Ford Jabbok may be very scary and it's certainly quiet and lonely but when He changes you and blesses you, there is not a wealthier place known to man.

I wish I had the paper and ink to write to you the wonderful things He has done for me these past few years.

This Ford Jabbok is where our Heavenly Father sends His Holy Spirit to prepare us to carry His Gospel to mankind. We must be changed to be like Him in humility, love and compassion.

2 Peter 1:4
"Whereby are given unto us exceeding great and precious promises: that by these ye might be partakers of the divine nature..."

Remember: You won't stay at the Ford Jabbok forever but stay until He blesses you and most important of all until he changes you! Then you'll be ready to move on and into the special place He has prepared for you.

Refined
Elayne Hawkins

Now when Job was tried and tested
He knew that all along
He was being tempered
For something better yet to come
So remember what Job told us
When the valley seems so cold
He said that when He hath tried me
I'll come forth as gold.

We must be refined
We must be refined
He wants a church that's set apart
He's coming for the pure, the pure in heart
So let the power of the Holy Ghost
Purify you for the Lord of Hosts
And when it's all said and done
Then you will be refined.

Now there have been some dark times
And there have been some cloudy days
But now I can say I understand
When trials come my way
For even in those dark times
This promise I am told
He said when he hath tried me
I'll come forth as gold.

Chapter 15

A Wealthy Place

"For thou, O God, hast proved us: thou hast tried us, as silver is tried. Thou broughtest us into the net; thou laidst affliction upon our loins. Thou hast caused men to ride over our heads; we went through fire and through water; but thou broughtest us out into a wealthy place."
(**Ps. 66:10-12**)

I'll never forget the night that the Lord gave me the above scriptures. The Sevilles were on our way to Fresno to do a concert. I opened my Bible to read and these words leaped off the page and into my spirit. The Holy Spirit began ministering to me that my Father had been ordering my steps all along and that He was bringing me into a wealthy place.

Immediately after the concert, a lady whom I'd never seen before came and said to me, "God wants me to give you this scripture." It was the same words (**Ps. 66:10-12**) that I had just read three hours before. He had confirmed His truth again.

I am absolutely convinced that **Rom. 8:28** holds all truth: "***And we know that all things work together for good to them that love God, to them who are the called according to his purpose.***" No one in the world could ever change my mind on this portion of scripture.

I can hear in my spirit now, as I am writing, some young lady saying, "How could that terrible abuse I had as a child work for my good? All it did was make me bitter. I'm still an emotional wreck."

Now, the promise of everything working for your good is only promised to those who love Him. Do you love Him? If the answer is yes, then let God bring you out of that furnace of affliction. You've been there long enough. Come on into a wealthy place. (***A wealthy place is where a sound mind, freedom from bitterness and confusion can be found***). When I came out of that furnace of fear years ago, my wealthy place was my sound mind and being able to enjoy life again. Let your past build great character in you.

Sir, the Spirit of the Lord is also prompting me that you're carrying a very private sin in your flesh. It has become a furnace to you. You have sought God many times to take it away from you but you keep returning to it. God would say to you, "Don't return to it return to Me." When the thing comes back to tempt and torment you, return to God and He will bring you from the furnace into a wealthy place. Can you just imagine how wonderful it would be to take those slave bands from off your neck and be free inside? No more inward shame! That's your wealthy place. It's yours! Receive it!

When your body is racked with pain daily and your health is nowhere in sight, you must see your health in your spirit by faith before you see it manifested in your life. Sickness is real furnace of affliction. People who have not experienced sickness day after day or sat in a wheelchair for years will never be able to know where you are coming from. Let your heavenly Father, while you're there, perfect you, establish you, strengthen you, and settle you, and bring you into your wealthy place.

To you, who are experiencing a broken heart because of divorce, after years of marriage to the same person, know that He can bring you into your wealthy place and into a new beginning.

Somebody said to me, after my husband and baby were gone, that "the glory of the later house would be greater than the former (**Haggai 2:9**). I said, "No, I don't want it greater. I love my home and family and the way it was. Even God couldn't give me something better than He gave me before." I was speaking through hurt. I didn't want change. So, I understand what you mean when you say, "NO, I don't want a new beginning."

Then I read the rest of the same verse that he had given me. It says, "Saith the Lord of Hosts: and in this place will I give peace." That's it! That's what you must have peace. It's His to give you and it's up to you whether you reject it or receive it.

I'd like to share with you in this final chapter about the wealthy places that my Father has brought me to. One great wealth is to see how Sara, has walked in remarkable strength. Her daddy didn't leave her a lot of money but he left her something greater: a strong faith and character.

Rick was a man of great strength and integrity. One neighbor rancher paid him a compliment to me one day saying, "Paulette, your husband is a Prince of a man. I'm always proud to stand beside him in a crowd."

Rick was very intelligent as well. Thank God, he also left that to Sara. My refrigerator is draped in her Honor Roll and Scholastic Achievement Awards. She is also a leader and not a follower. I'm thankful for this wealthy place.

Another place is to watch other lives changed because my family's lives took on so great a change. **Hebrews 11:4**, *"By it, he being dead yet speaketh".*

One night, about 1:00 in the morning, Jamie called me to her bedside, about one month before she went to be with the Lord. "Mom," she said, "I can't go to sleep." She had been thinking about a young man in her fifth grade class who gave her a real hard time. She said, "Mom, he cusses and swears and is so mean and when Jesus comes to get us he won't be saved." She began to cry and say, "Mama, can we pray for him? I don't want him to go to hell!"

So, we prayed for him and some of the other children as well. Her heart seemed to be breaking for this boy who had embarrassed her time after time. I stayed with her about an hour that night.

The next night, she called me to her room again. She said to me, "Mom, Jesus is coming real soon."

I said, "I know He is baby."

"But," she said, "He's coming real soon!" He must have been letting her know He was coming for her.

She said, "Mom, how can I know that I'm really ready to go with Him?" (Please dwell on this thought for a moment.)

"Jamie," I said, "you've invited Jesus into your heart and you've asked Him to forgive you of your sins, haven't you?"

She said, "Yes, Mom but how can I get hold of it?" It seemed that she just had to know. She said to me that she knew the difference between good and evil and that she was at the age of accountability. She was saying that now she was old enough and understood enough and was required to make her choice between heaven or hell.

I have trophies in my office that belong to Jamie for memorizing the scriptures. That night, I questioned her, "Honey, what must you do to be saved?" She quoted the scripture and verse to me (**Rom. 10:9**); "*That if thou shalt confess with thy mouth the Lord Jesus, and shalt believe in thine heart that God hath raised Him from the dead, thou shalt be saved.*" As quickly as I could ask her questions, she would answer with words from the Bible.

I said, "Jamie, so you will know that you are ready to meet Jesus, should He come tonight, let's pray again asking His forgiveness and inviting Him into your heart." After we prayed, she was satisfied.

I then held her awhile, thinking how pure and precious she was. Before she fell asleep, she said, "Mom, let me share with you the latest scriptures Sis. Hearne helped me to memorize. She quoted the words from Jesus in **John 14:3**: "*Let not your heart be troubled: ye believe in God, believe also in me. In my Father's house are many mansions: if it were not so, I would have told you. I go to prepare a place for you. And if I go and prepare a place for you, I will come again, and receive you unto myself; that where I am, there ye may be also.*"

With that, she fell asleep, assured she was ready to meet Jesus. How these two special moments with my precious little one in the middle of the night comforted me when she was gone.

Months later, we were ministering in a church one Sunday morning and the Lord told me to preach on "Out of the Mouth of Babes" (**Ps. 8:2**). I shared Jamie's sermon she had given me during our moments together those nights. When five adult men and one woman came to the altar and received Jesus after the sermon, I saw my wealthy place again.

Wealth of a Dream

When I felt as though I didn't have the wisdom to answer Jamie's question, the Lord came to help me. He quickly helped me to answer Sara's questions as well after her sister was gone.

One night, Sara said to me, "Mommy, I would like to ask Daddy and Jamie how they like their new home. I dream about Dad but every time I get near him, he disappears."

I had no idea what to say to my little girl. I knew she couldn't talk to her Dad in a dream, but I didn't want to discourage her in telling her so, but understand, the Holy Spirit heard our conversation.

Two nights later, He allowed me to have a dream that answered her questions in every detail. In the dream, I was sitting on the little white corral fence in front of our red barn-style house. As I looked toward the driveway, I saw Rick and another rancher standing there talking. They both had on their 4" brim white hats. Now Rick was walking my way and I went to meet him. My first question was, "Honey, how do you like Heaven?"

He spoke in his soft, gentle voice, "Babe, it is so wonderful, earth has no words to describe it." He said to me, "We were so blessed to be chosen to come."

Now, notice he said, "We" but Jamie wasn't with him. The words "blessed" and "chosen" were spoken in another tongue but I understood by the Spirit.

Then I asked him as a wife, something very important to me> "Honey, do you and Jamie miss us?"

He said, "No, there is none of that there." Then he started to walk away.

I yelled, "Wait a minute. I want to ask you one more thing."

He said, very sternly to me, "That's all for today." With that, he left and walked away.

I could no longer see the other rancher but how I felt His presence! I knew that he was a heavenly being set to escort Rick to me during this divine visitation. The question I was going to ask Rick before he left me was, "What do you want me to do with all these cattle?" I said to him in the dream as he walked away, "It's great for you there but it's the pits down here, making all these decisions alone."

But, God became by business partner as well and He helped me to make quality decisions. He helped me to finish out the lease at the ranch. He showed me what I must do to have the cattle cared for and when to move.

When Sara and I awoke in the morning after the dream, how she delighted in hearing how her daddy enjoyed his new home! It was also very comforting to us to know they didn't miss us.

One evening Sara was sitting in the bathtub alone. She and her sister used to bathe together so I went in to keep her company. I was feeling kind of low and she could sense something was wrong. "What's wrong with you, Mom?" She asked.

I replied, "I guess I miss Dad and Jamie tonight."

She said, recalling my dream, "why do you miss them? They don't miss us."

Oh, the wealthy places are great blessings.

My Husband Ishi

In April of 1988, I went to a women's retreat in Oklahoma City. In the hotel one night the Lord dropped this scripture into my heart. **Hosea 2:16,** *"**And it shall be at that day, saith the Lord, that thou shalt call me Ishi: and shalt call me no more Baali.**"* In other words, you shall call me Husband (Ishi) and thou shalt no more call me Lord (Baali). This was wonderful to me.

I have promised my Husband (Ishi) that I will do what He has called me to do until He comes for me or calls me home. I also promised to love and cherish Him, in sickness and in health, for richer or poorer, for better or worse, until He comes for me.

There seemed to be some kind of shame that came with widowhood. I couldn't put my finger on it but I didn't like it. What a furnace widowhood could be! Could He bring me to a wealthy place here?

He is so sweet to answer our questions. I saw the comfort I needed in **Isaiah 54:4-5,** *"**Fear not: for though shalt not be ashamed: neither be though confounded; for thou shalt not be put to shame: for thou shalt forget the shame of thy youth, and shalt no remember the reproach of thy widowhood any more. For thy maker is thing husband (Ishi); the Lord of Hosts is His name.**"*

You widows and widowers get hold of this. He will become your closest companion. He meets every one of my needs. He knows how to lift the frustration of widowhood off your body, soul and spirit. My Ishi (husband) makes this possible.

Jesus made me a whole woman. I knew how it feels when that one flesh is torn apart. Its pain is total agony at times but when you become intimate with Jesus, He will do more than fill in the gap. He brings you to the wealthy place of wholeness. You will no longer feel like a third wheel unless you choose to. You will not feel like half a person when He brings you to the wealthy place.

Many times when I'm out ministering, I will sit at a table with the pastors and three or four couples and not feel like I am out of place. When you get past that emptiness, it's a wealthy place. I feel this because my husband, (Ishi,) is not just beside me but He is in me.

A New Beginning

The place that I didn't want to be is now a blessing to me. The ranch life, a family of four and a noisy home is all behind me now. It was perfect for then and the place I'm in now is perfect for now.

The Lord allowed Sara and me to have a home built after living with Elayne and Doyle for a year. We chose all our own colors for this house and did it the way we wanted to. It was so wonderful for us to have our privacy again. There was a lot of adjusting to our new life-style but we have learned to love and enjoy our lives together.

During the furnace, Sara had a hard time leaving me even to go to school. To be honest, I had a tough time as well. I wouldn't allow us to be split up and travel in different cars because of fear.

How wonderful it is since he's brought us to our wealthy place. Sara goes to school and never complains and has many friends. She's even gone to two slumber parties and I even stayed at home alone! How God helped us move right on in to our wealthy place. The thought of fear will still try to come against us at times but we cast them down together.

The Ministry, the wealthiest place.

I was ordained to preach in 1988. I knew I was called from an early age but I must tell what Jesus had done for me. There is nothing in this life that compares to the anointing of His Holy Spirit.

God has given me many songs that have brought deliverance to many. Along with Elayne and Doyle, we have been recording in Nashville every year and have traveled many miles. These songs have carried a special anointing. I've seen and heard testimonies of how the songs brought deliverance and encouragement.

One man in particular, one night was listening to our tape when it broke the spirit of suicide over him.

I met a grieving lady at a retreat who shared with me how she would drink and drive but how God had delivered her through my song, "He's Coming For Me." *Again the anointing breaks the yokes.* **Isaiah 10:27, "And it shall come to pass in that day, that his burden shall be taken away from off thy shoulder, and His yoke from off thy neck, and the yoke shall be destroyed because of the anointing."** The anointing on the ministry has so increased as we have decreased.

The greatest of all the wealthy places has been to watch men, women, boys and girls whose lives have been set free and changed by the power of God. We've seen many healings, both emotional and physical, in every city we've gone. I've seen hundreds healed emotionally – leaving a tormenting past and entering God's Recovery Room, escaping the ugliness. **Ps. 124:7,** ***"Our soul is escaped as a bird out of the snare of the fowlers: the snare is broken, and we are escaped."***

Not only has He freed me but he has used the circumstances of my life to free others. His plan was so perfect in our lives.

1. <u>Jesus gave me peace</u> inner tranquility in a situation wanting attention.
2. <u>Jesus gave me light</u> in the impenetrable darkness.
3. <u>Jesus gave me calm assurance</u> in impossible circumstances.
4. <u>Jesus gave me unexplainable rest</u> in the midst of chaos. (Thank God, He has brought me out of the furnace and into a wealthy place.) I am in a wealthy place.

These four blessings run with the furnace of affliction and a most wonderful blessing waits just around the corner for you.

I kept telling Sara from the very beginning, "Honey, expect great things."

"What kind of things, Mommy?"

"I don't know, baby just great things."

Is. 61:1, ***"The Spirit of the Lord God is upon me; because the Lord hath anointed me to preach good tidings unto the meek; He hath sent me to bind up the brokenhearted, to proclaim liberty to the captives, and the opening of the prison to them that are bound."***

While in prayer and fasting one week the Lord revealed this word to me.

There will be a day of riotous, contentious living. Only those trained in My army will survive, well trained soldiers.

You are the one chosen to deliver the message I have given. Yea, and I say go and give. Thou art a worthy yielded vessel. Thou hast walked with Me many days and I with you.

The day will come when men and women, My men and women, will deny Me and say they never knew Me; so I will turn them over to it. The handwriting will be on the wall; yea, My handwriting for them to see as did Belshazar, the king. You shall be My Daniel to bring them My news. I must raise up many other Daniels who will be willing to suffer lions' dens and fiery furnaces to see My power and glory, saith God. Yes, he who suffers with Me will reign with Me, both now and then.

I call My people now, away from feasting to fasting, saith God, that all will be ready for My kingdom.

Go ye, therefore, and teach all nations. Go, go, go.

My Spirit wind is beginning to blow upon thee, Expect great exploits by My name and power.

You will carry a fresh, new message of the Holy Ghost, and His power and signs and wonders will follow. Because I have chosen you for the task, walk in power and in My Spirit, yea, full of My Spirit, saith God.

The Beginning

EPILOGUE

You will notice as you read the last words of this book it says "The Beginning", instead of The End.

Somehow I knew in my heart that this was a new beginning, not just for Rick and Jamie, but for Sara and I.

After the accident I spent the next 9 years in full time ministry, crisscrossing the United States with my sister and brother-in-law. Many awesome doors were opened and the power of Jesus was constantly upon us.

The Lord directed us back to our home town of Porterville, California, where I founded a church. Landmark Christian Center (LCC). God has favored us here at Landmark these past 20 years.

We also began a two-year Bible College. Landmark Bible Insitute.
And, Landmark Christian Acadamy, grades K-8.

My Sara is now a Radiation Therapist for the local Cancer Center. She married a wonderful Christian man David Smith, an Engineer at the City Fire Department and they have two beautiful children. Ainsley and Parker, which I might add are the joys of my life.

God has truly brought us to a "Wealthy Place"

www.ingramcontent.com/pod-product-compliance
Lightning Source LLC
Chambersburg PA
CBHW070856050426
42453CB00012B/2227